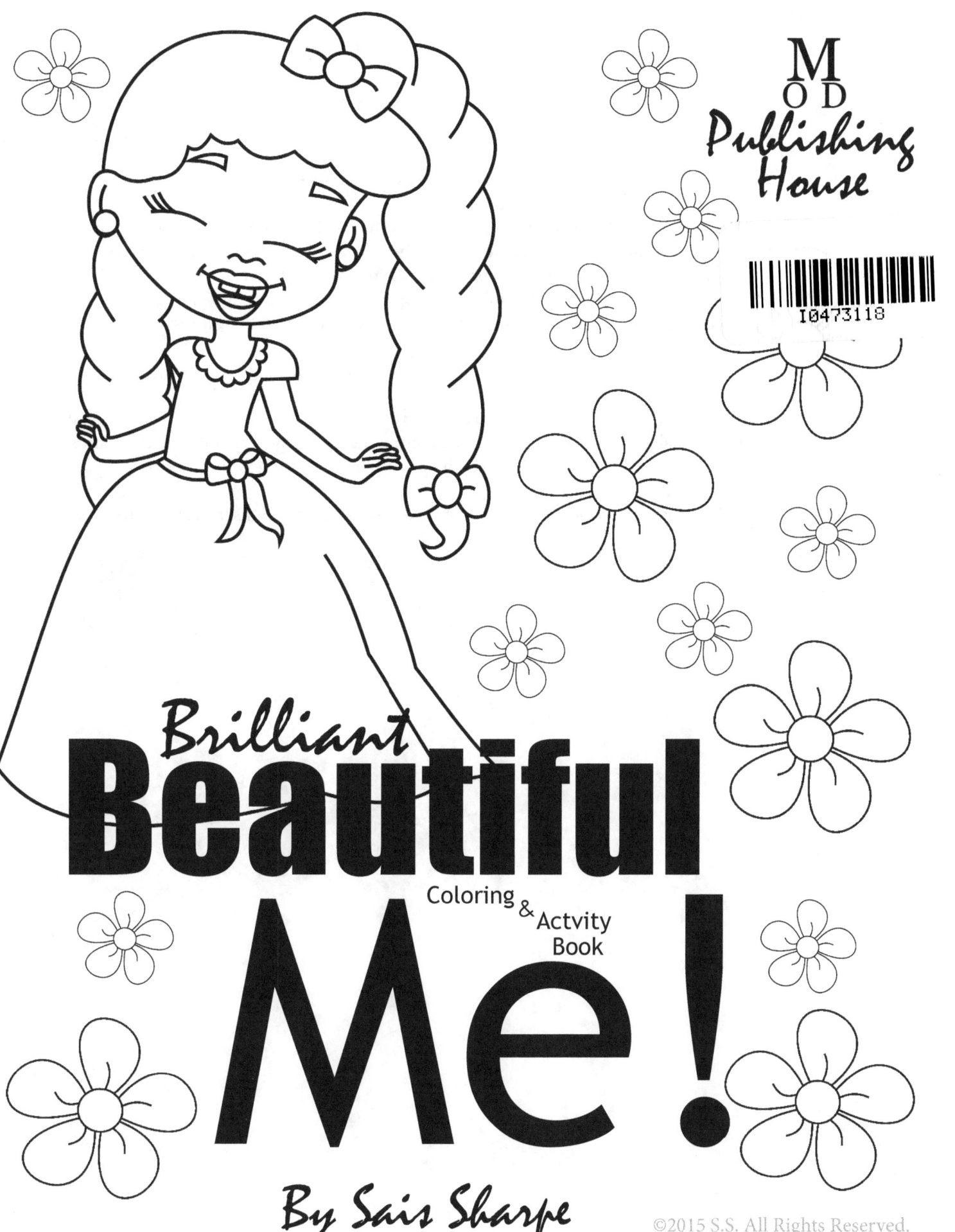

Modpublishinghouse@yahoo.com

Ordering Information:
Quantity sales. Special discounts are available on quantity purchases by corporations, associations, and others. For details, contact the publisher at the address above.

Brilliant Beautiful Me! : Coloring & Activity Book / Illustrations by Sais Sharpe

ISBN 978-0-9898403-3-0

First Edition

To my Brilliant & Beautiful Princess Milly. Mama loves you!

I would also like to dedicate this book to girls all over the world, of all shades and ages. You are Brilliant and you are Beautiful!

~Sais S.

This book belongs to

_____

{Write your _beautiful_ name on the line above.}

_____

Presented by

_____

Date

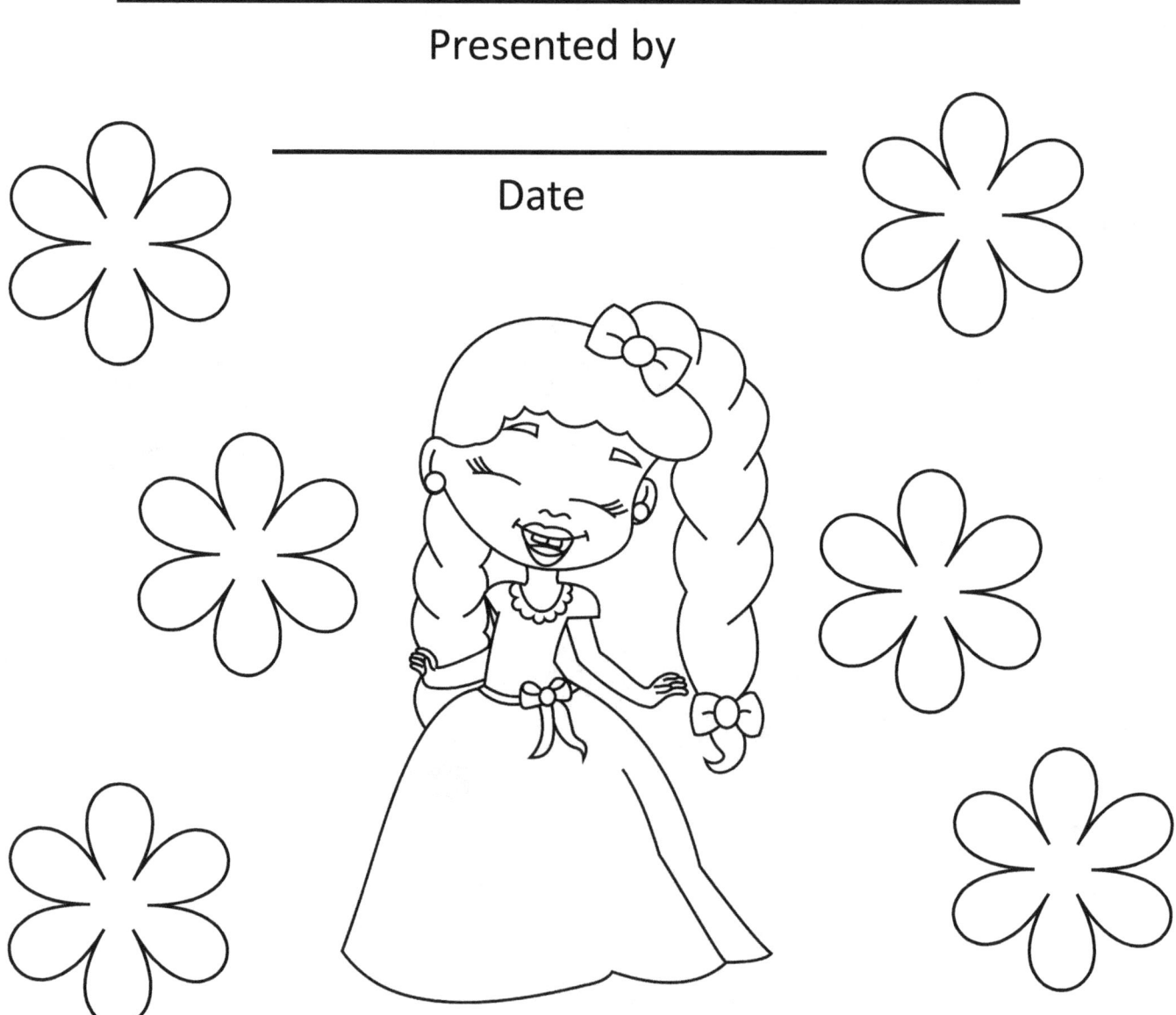

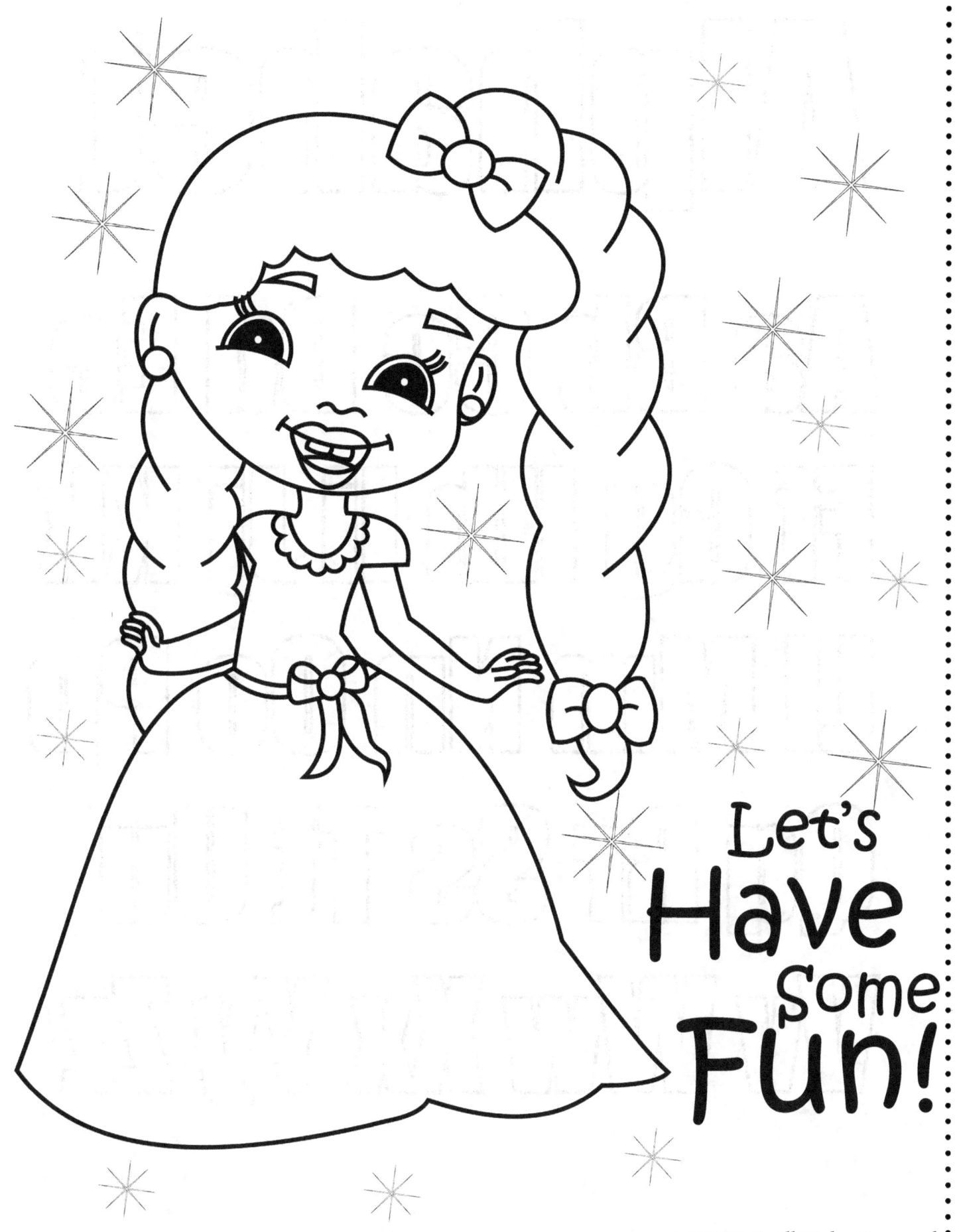

Let's
Have
Some
Fun!

Alphabet

Aa Bb Cc Dd Ee
Ff Gg Hh Ii Jj Kk
Ll Mm Nn Oo Pp
Qq Rr Ss Tt Uu
Vv Ww Xx Yy Zz

Bird

Cupcakes

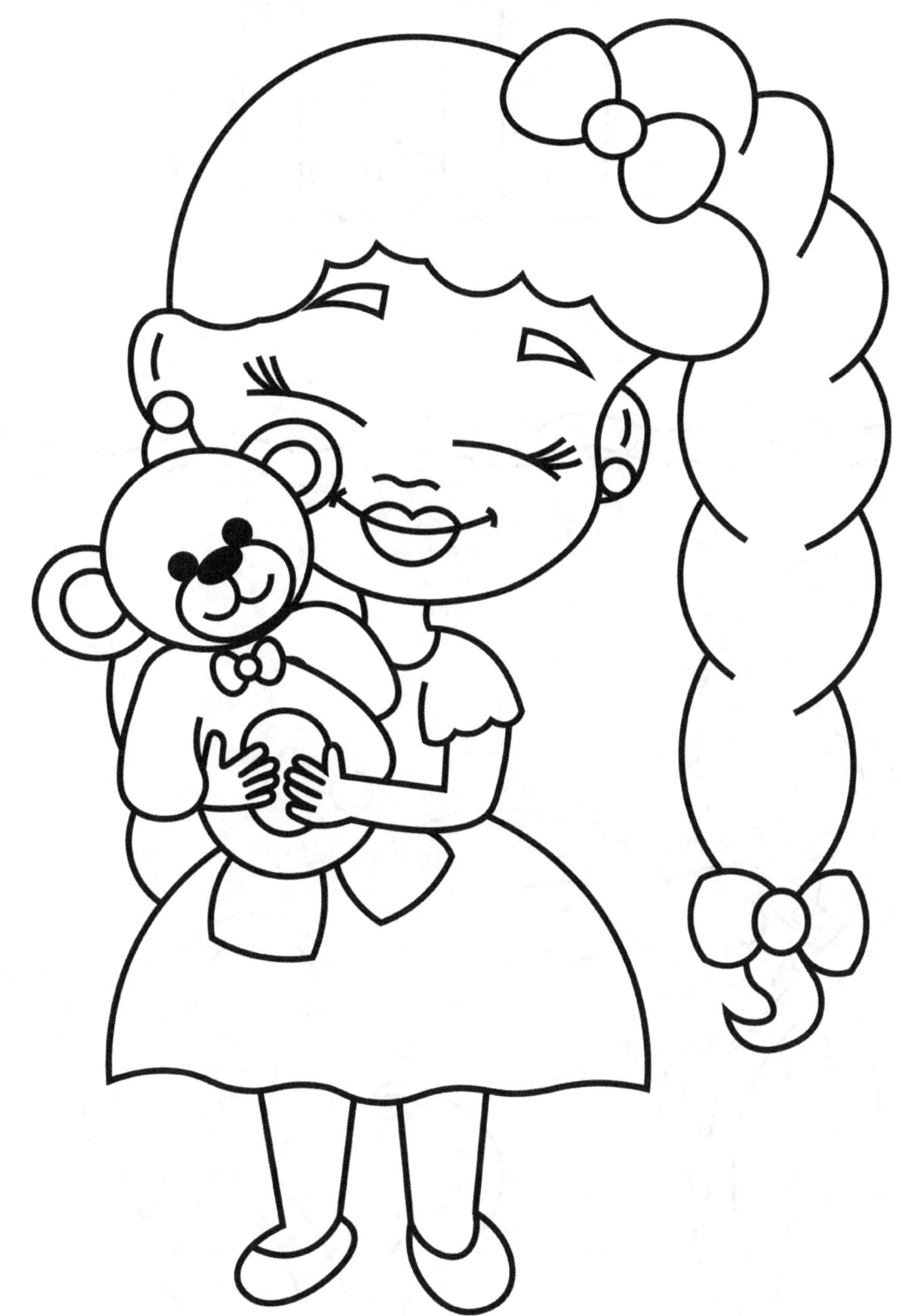

Mr. Bear loves hugs!

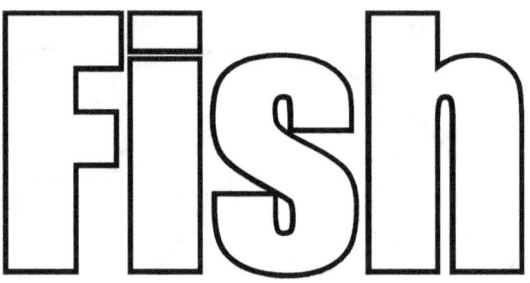

Fish

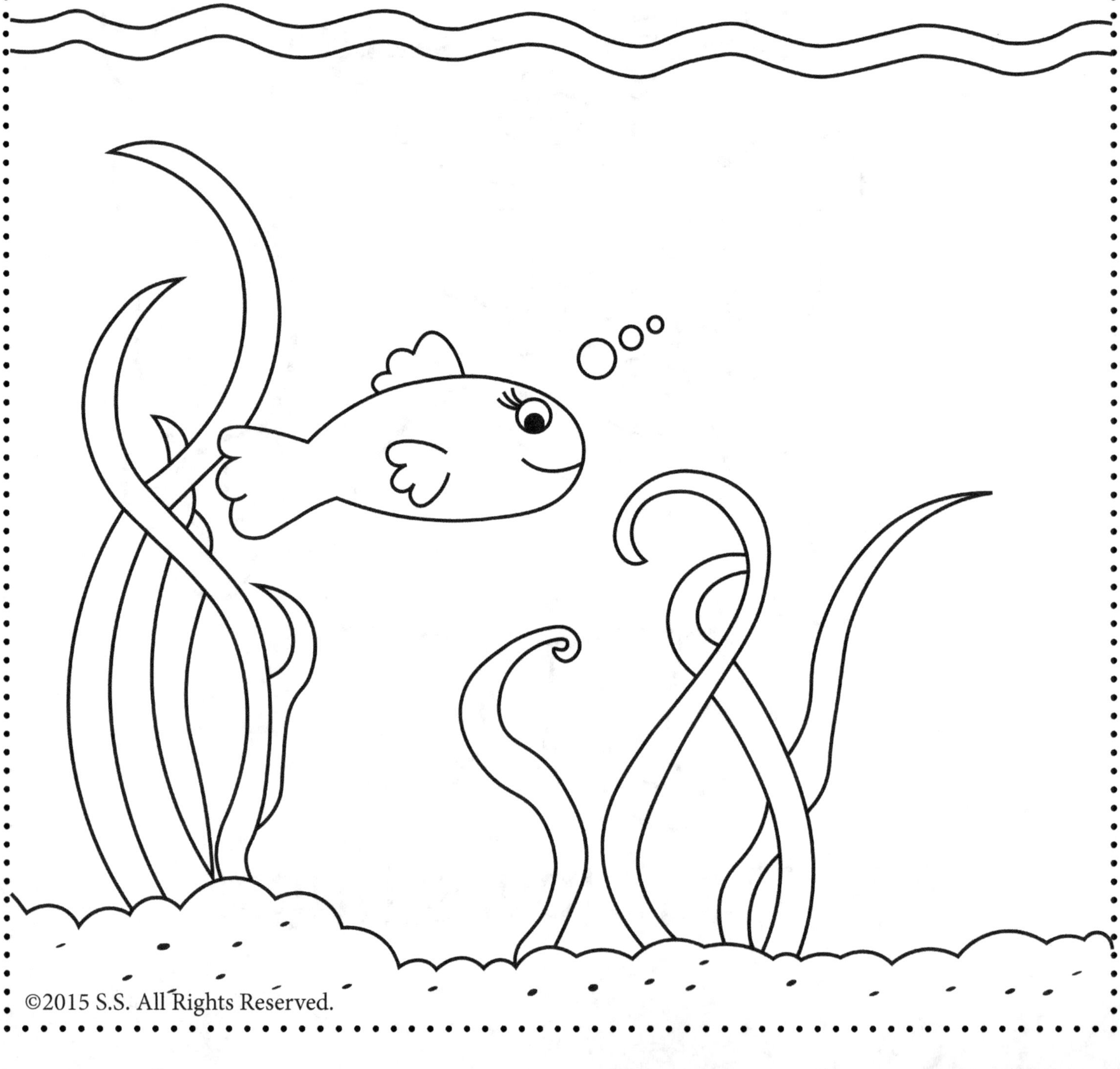

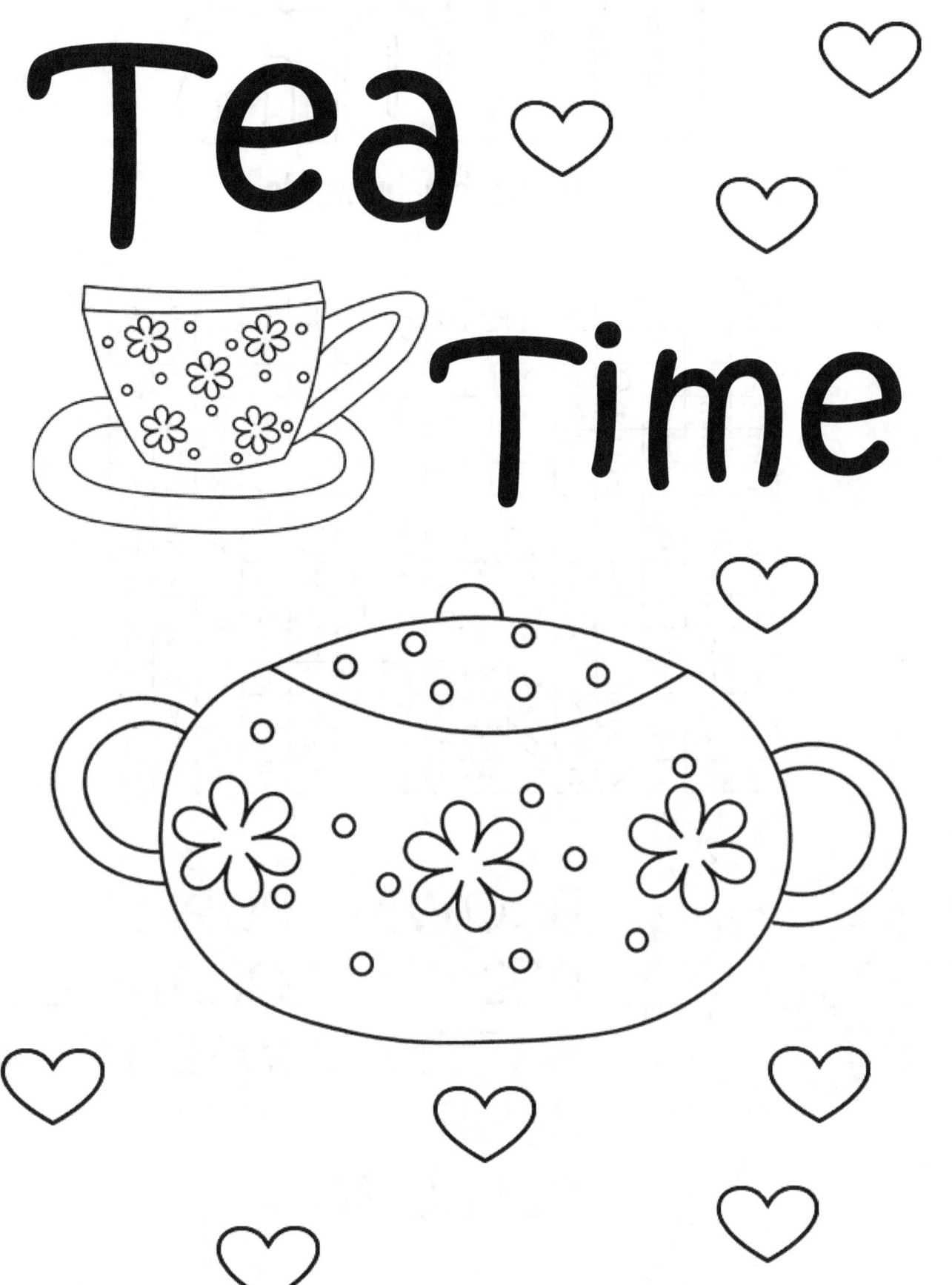

Colors

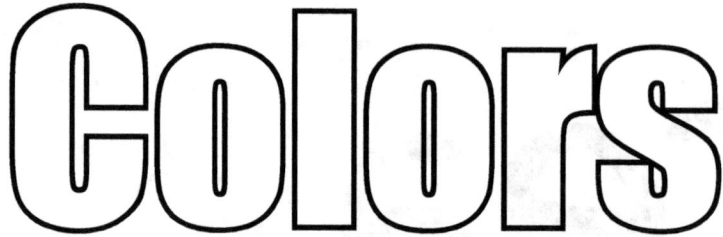

Find the hidden words.

W	N	J	J	N	Q	P	U	R	P	L	E	K	J	R
H	V	Q	M	B	D	V	G	Q	I	F	Q	N	V	Y
I	D	T	Q	X	P	N	Z	L	W	A	F	T	R	O
T	E	L	B	G	G	F	L	U	Y	T	G	N	D	S
E	F	B	C	R	B	U	H	P	D	P	Y	S	J	V
E	F	Y	T	E	L	K	V	O	U	N	E	B	Z	B
N	W	U	A	E	V	R	J	D	Q	P	L	B	D	L
U	O	R	A	N	G	E	T	O	I	W	L	P	K	U
G	V	V	V	I	Y	H	B	A	B	R	O	W	N	E
W	T	A	X	Q	O	X	H	S	L	X	W	T	M	D
I	U	R	P	O	V	U	B	R	A	R	P	H	R	V
L	U	I	O	Z	S	Z	E	P	C	E	L	Q	M	G
L	G	X	W	C	W	M	D	X	K	D	C	V	V	V
X	I	T	F	P	C	M	A	M	P	N	H	O	L	A
Y	K	T	K	C	C	M	Y	B	E	T	V	S	I	M

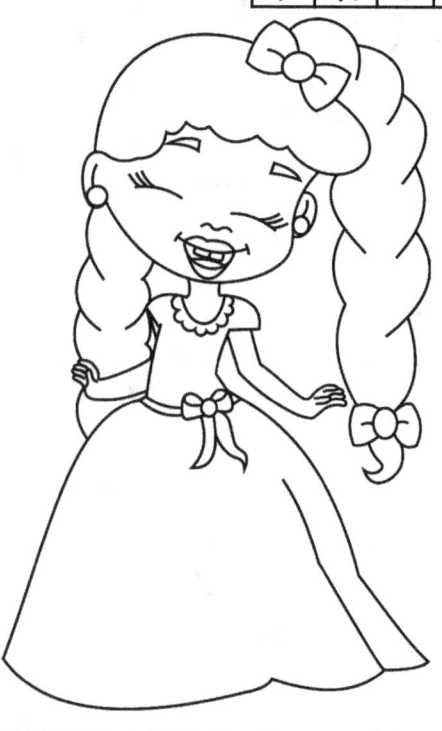

BROWN   PURPLE

RED   ORANGE

GREEN   WHITE

BLUE

YELLOW

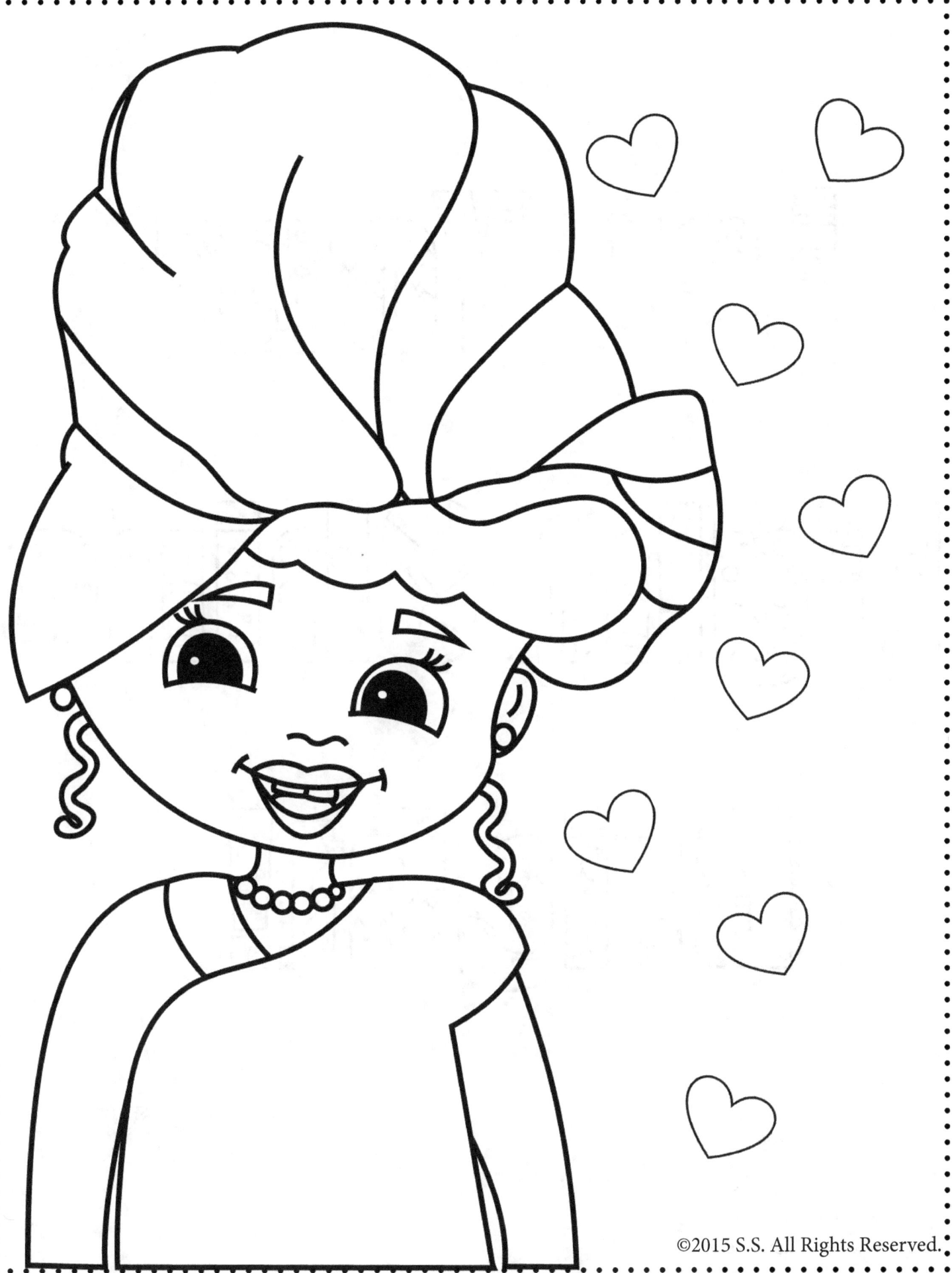

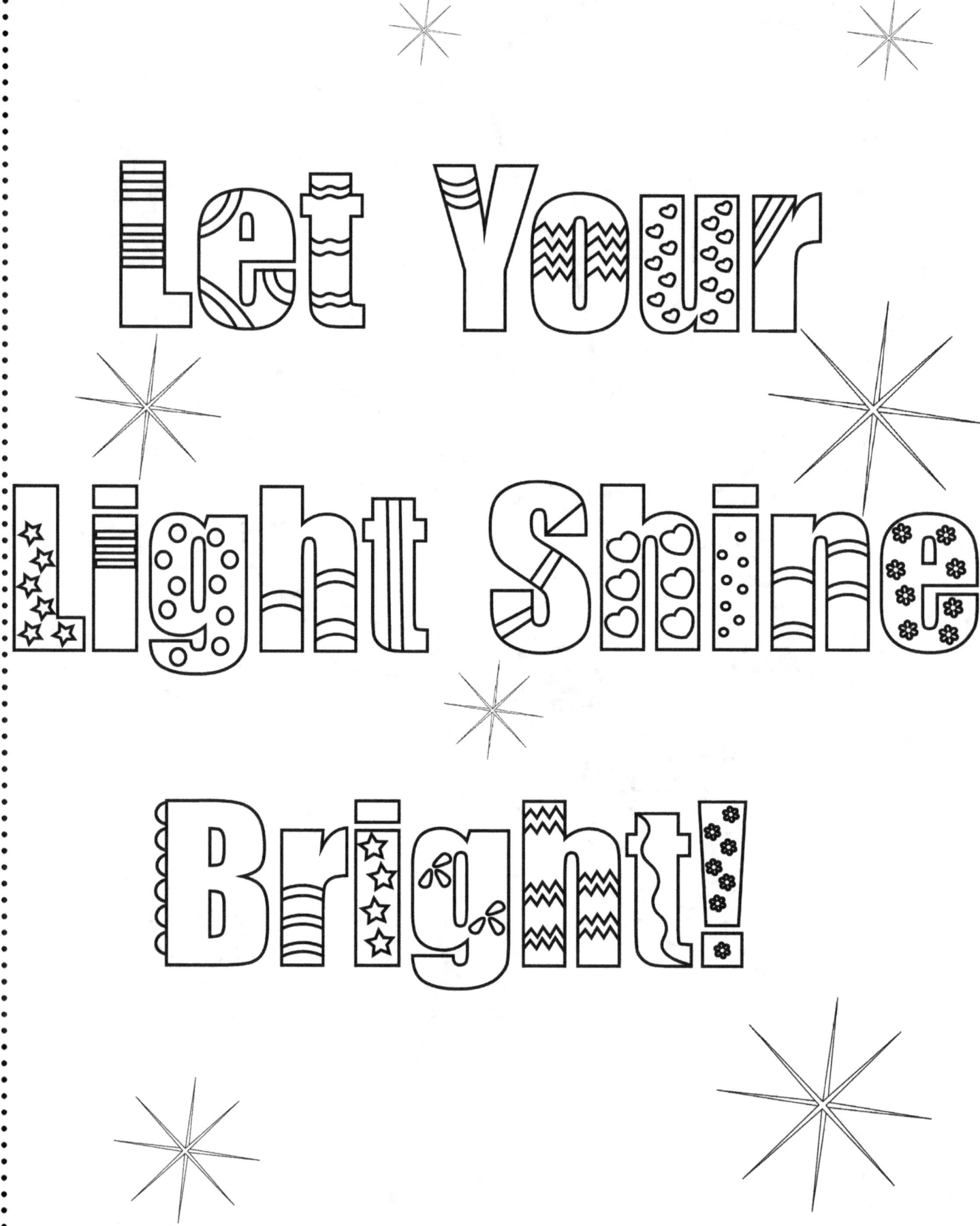

Backpack

Addition

Add the flowers.

❀ + ❀ = _____

1   1

❀ ❀ + ❀ = _____

2   1

❀ ❀ ❀ + ❀ = _____

3   1

Bows

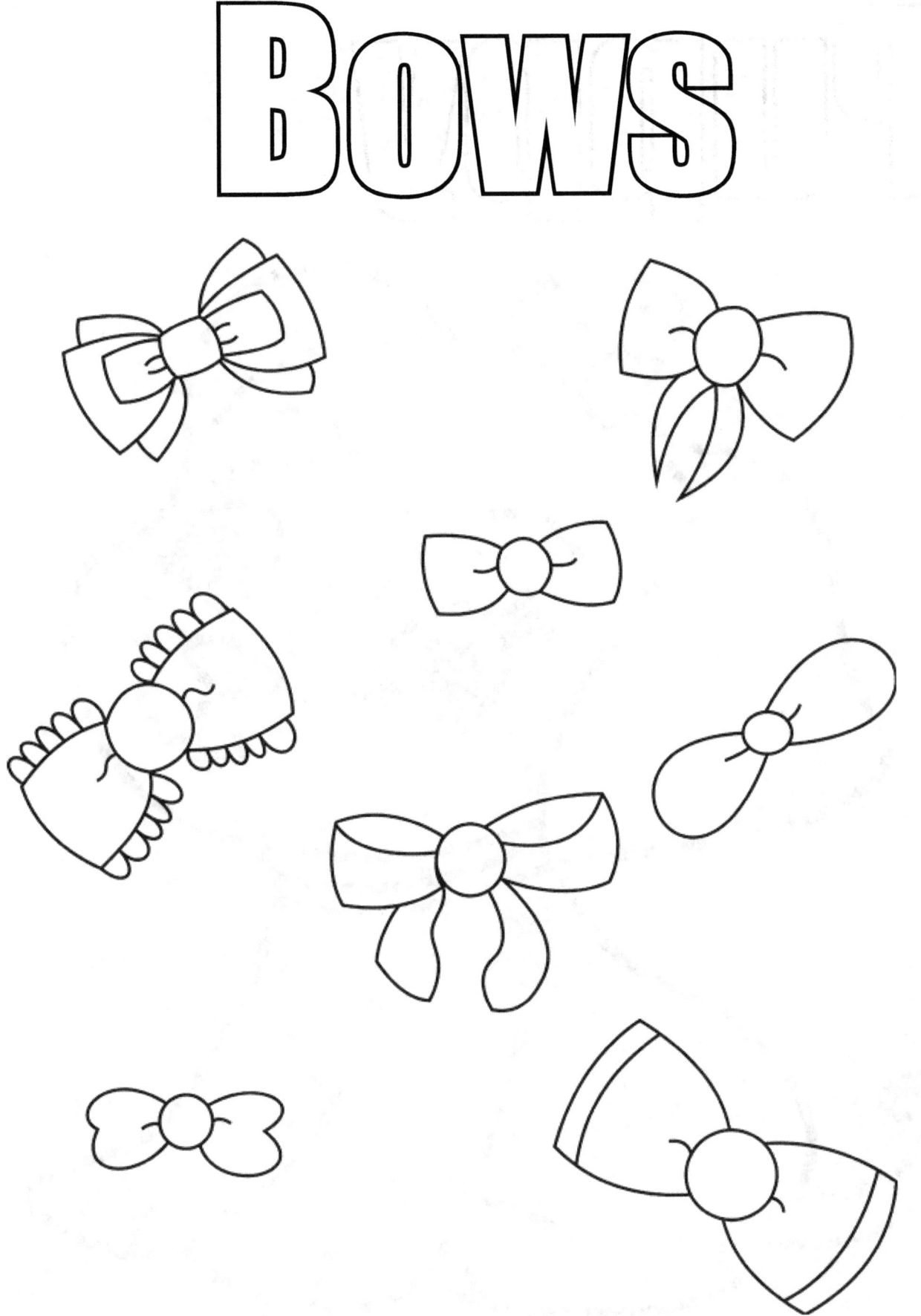

Puppy

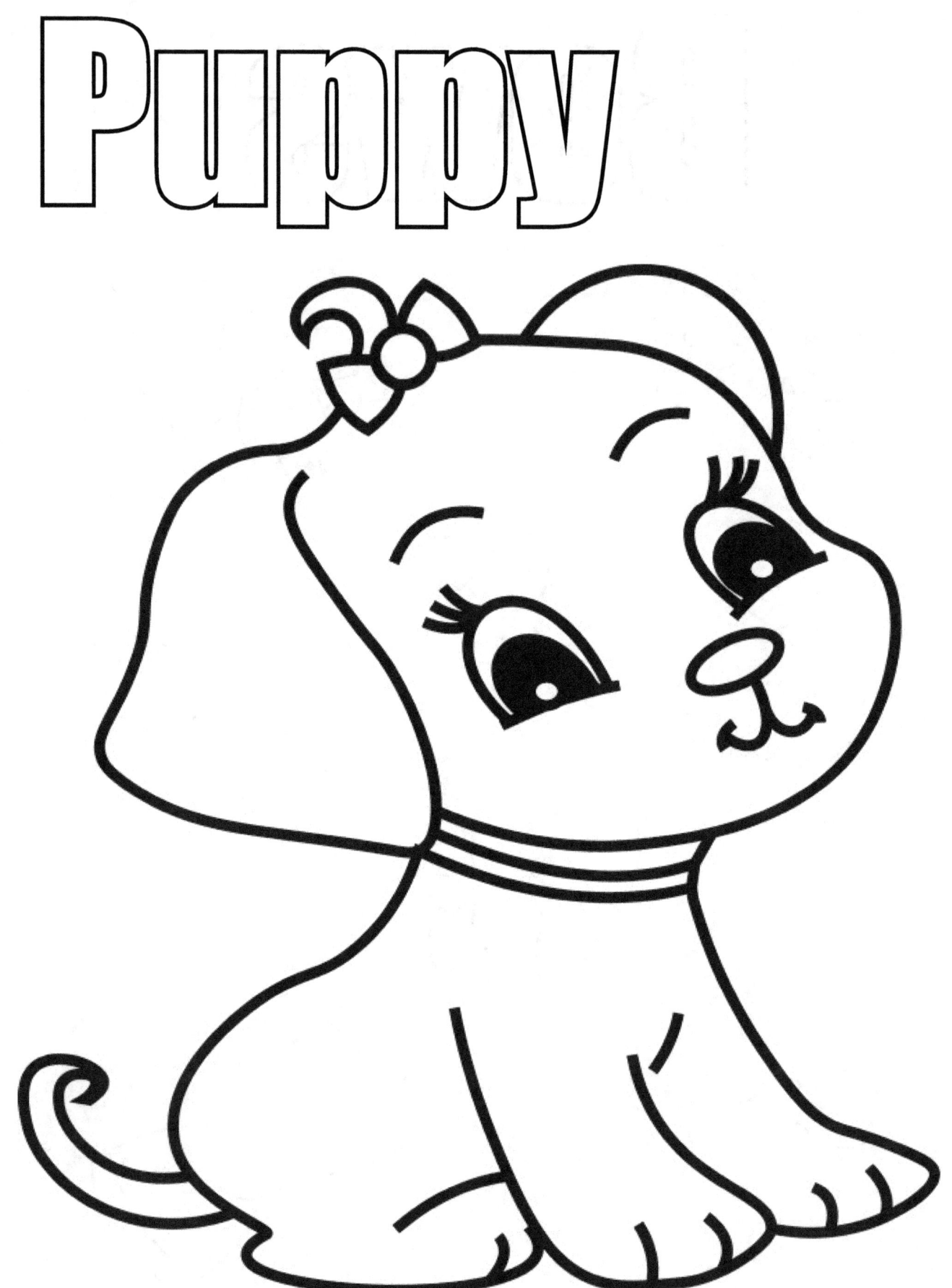

I am brilliant.

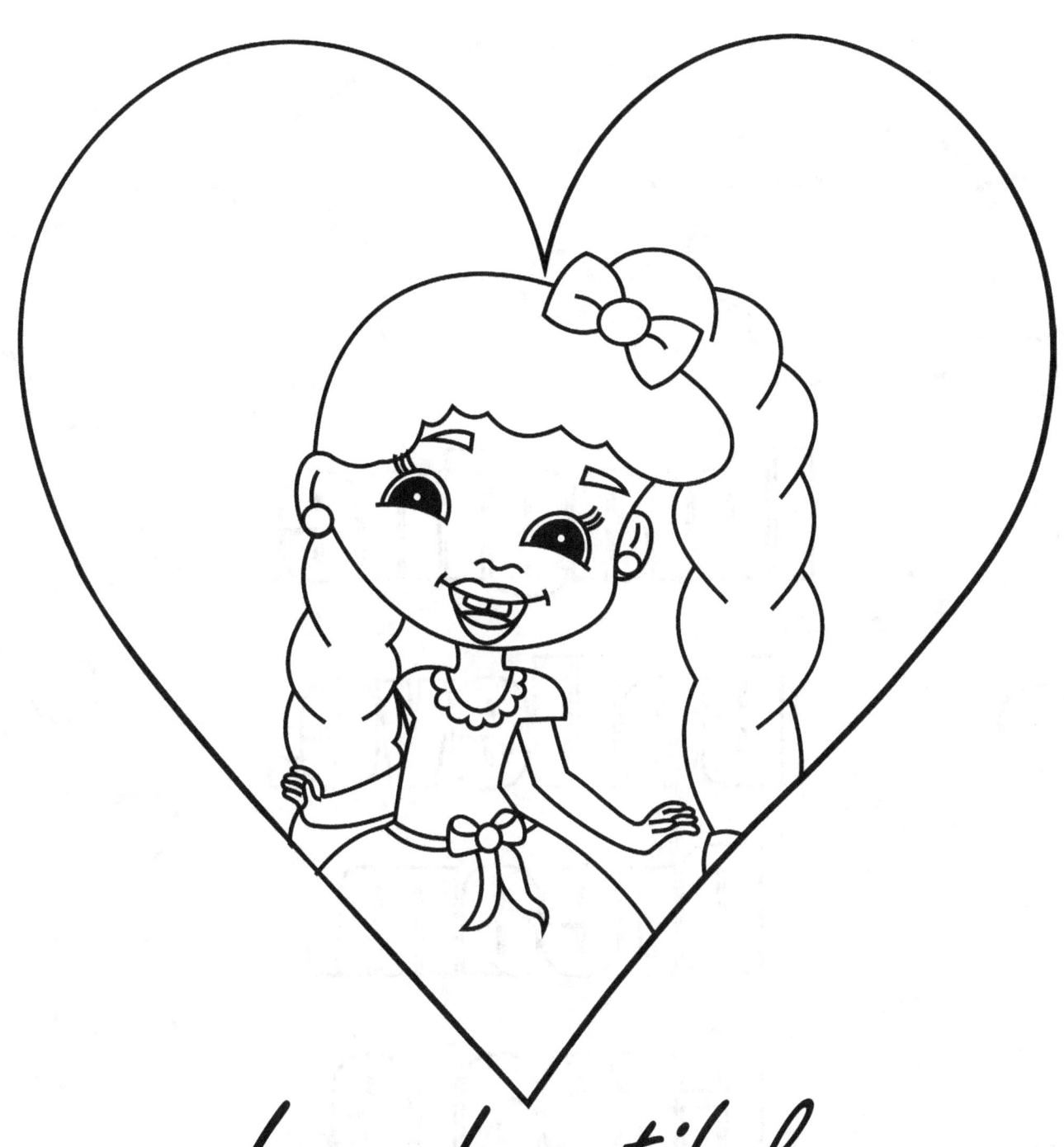

I am beautiful.

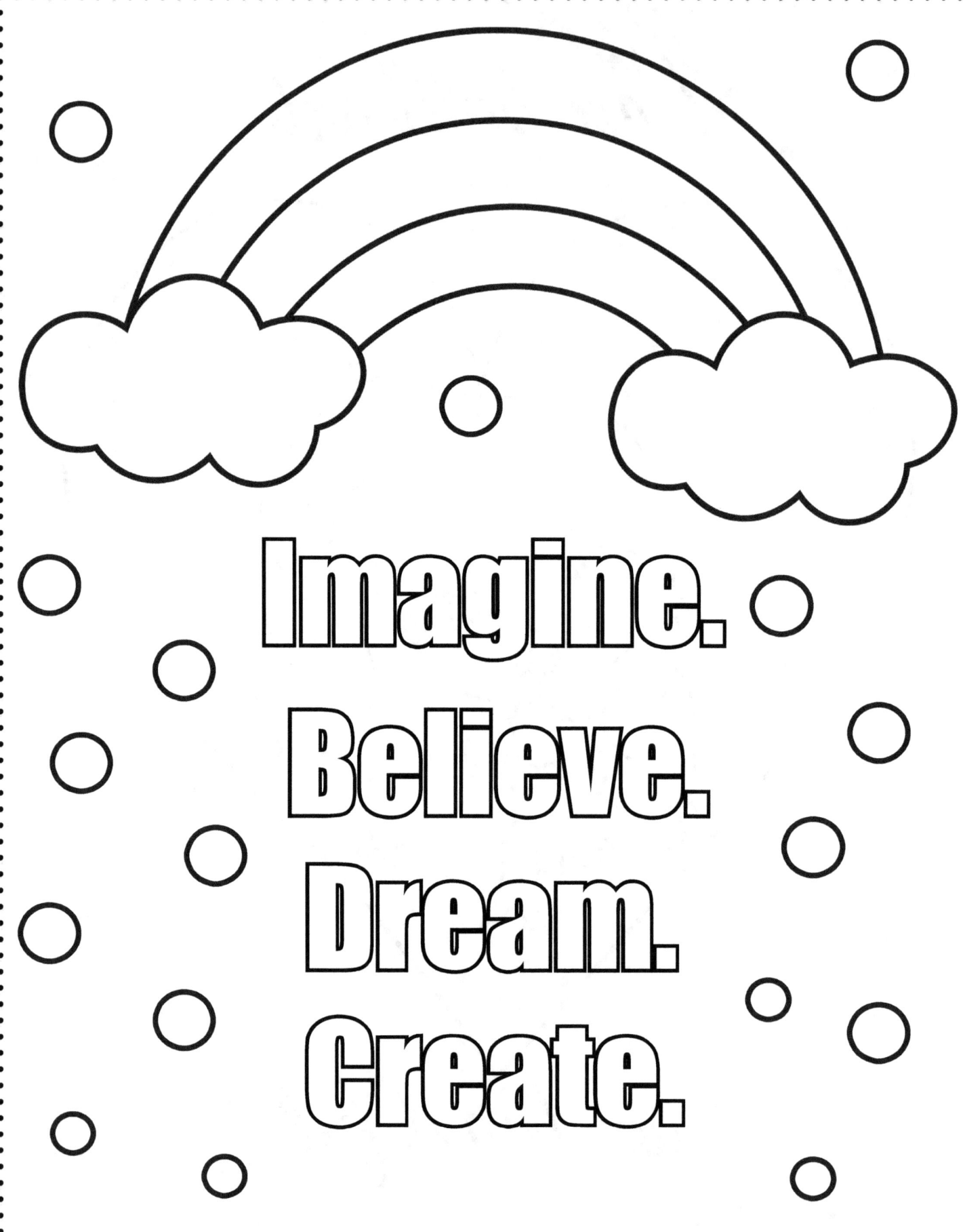

Imagine.
Believe.
Dream.
Create.

Numbers

0 1 2 3

4 5 6 7

8 9

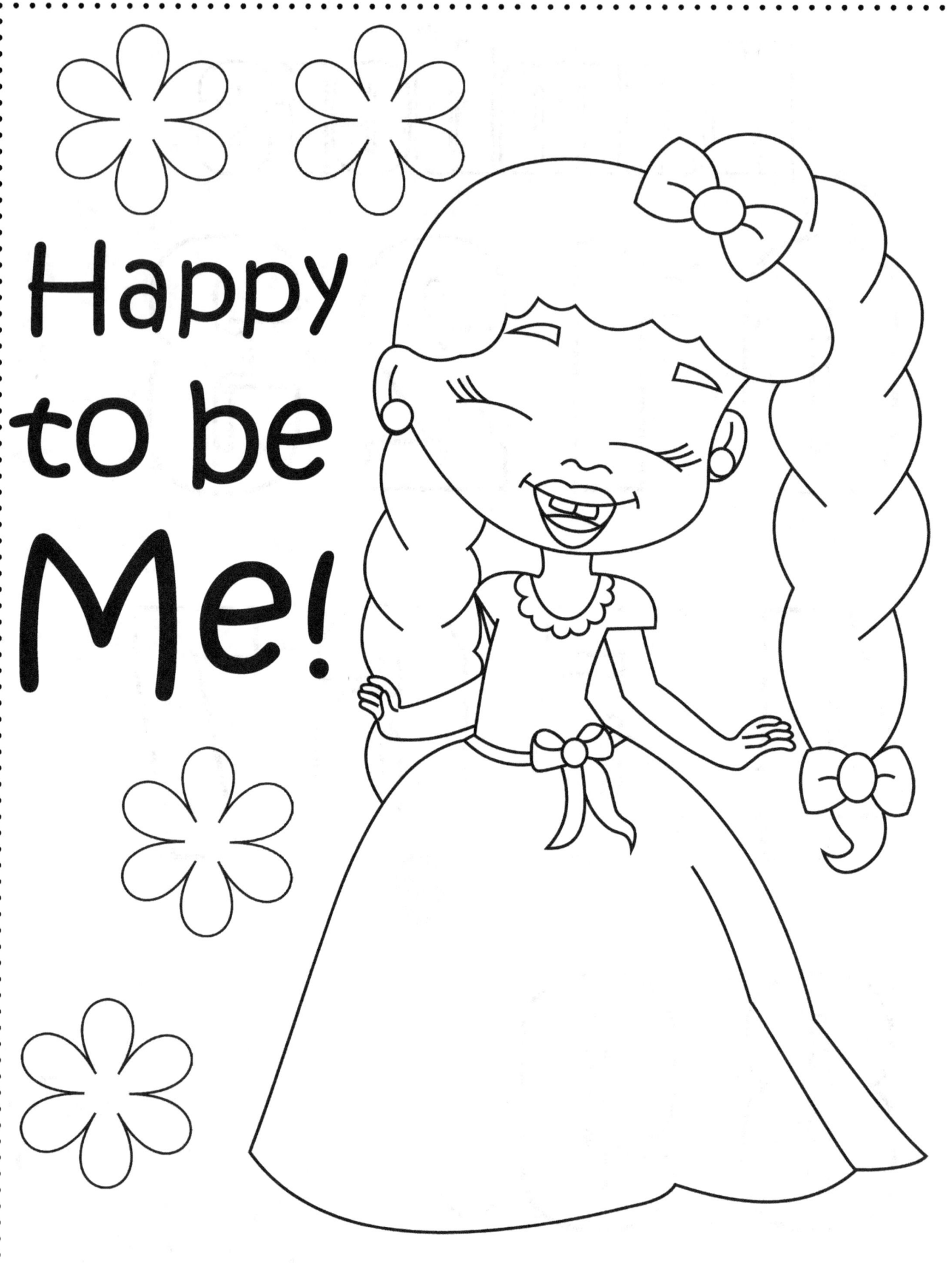

Happy
to be
Me!

Notebook & Pencil

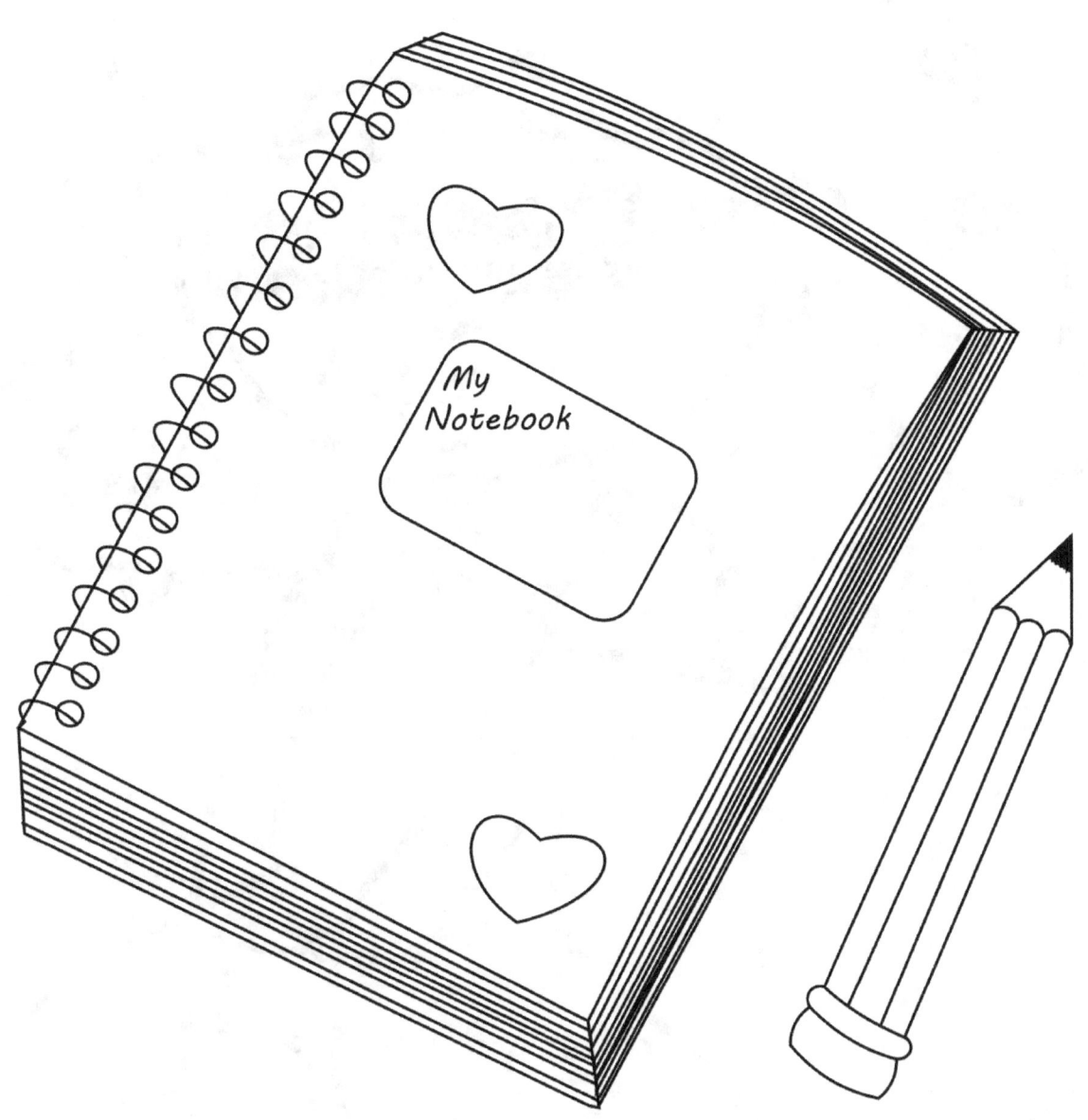

My
Notebook

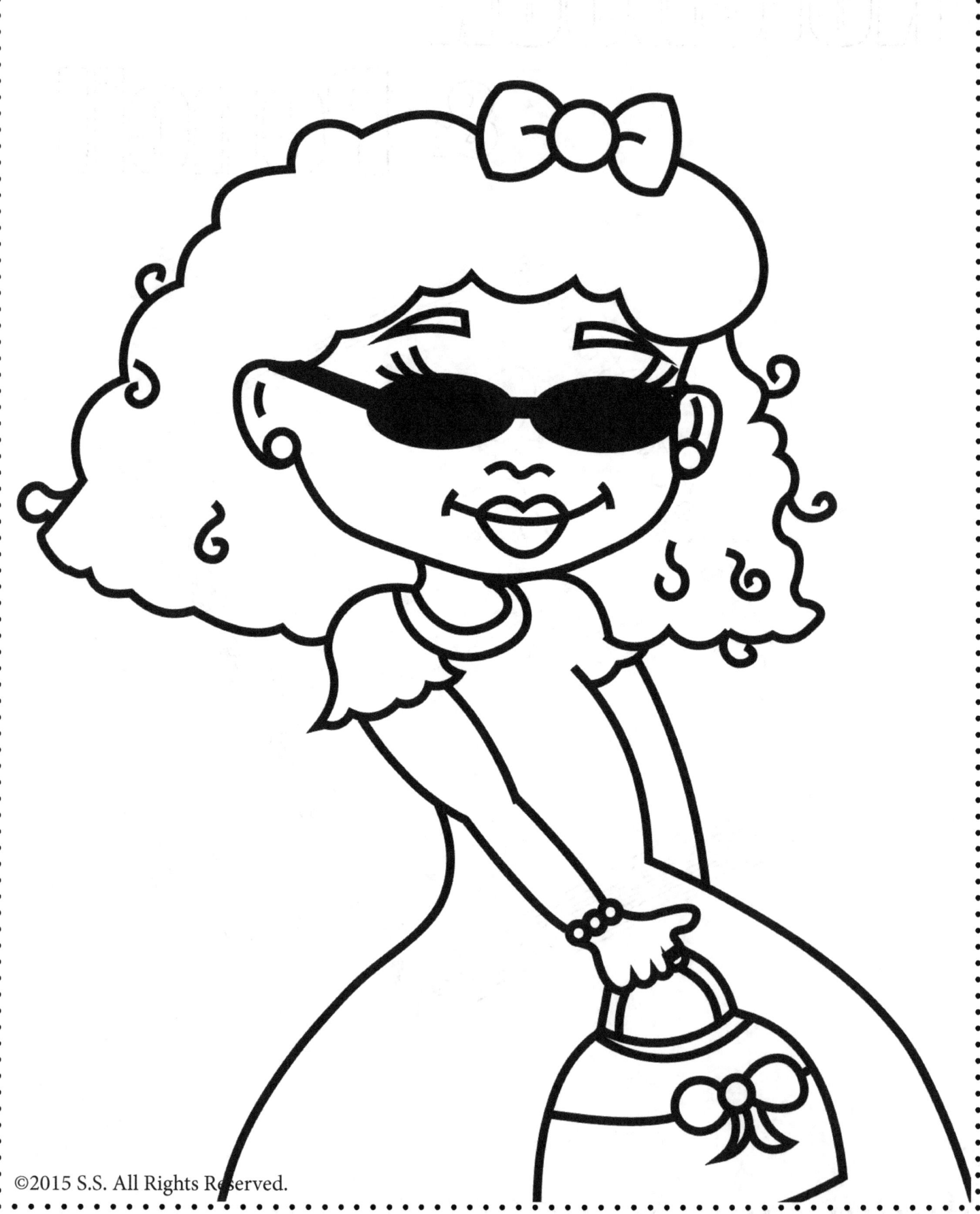

My Drawing

Draw a picture of yourself inside the mirror!

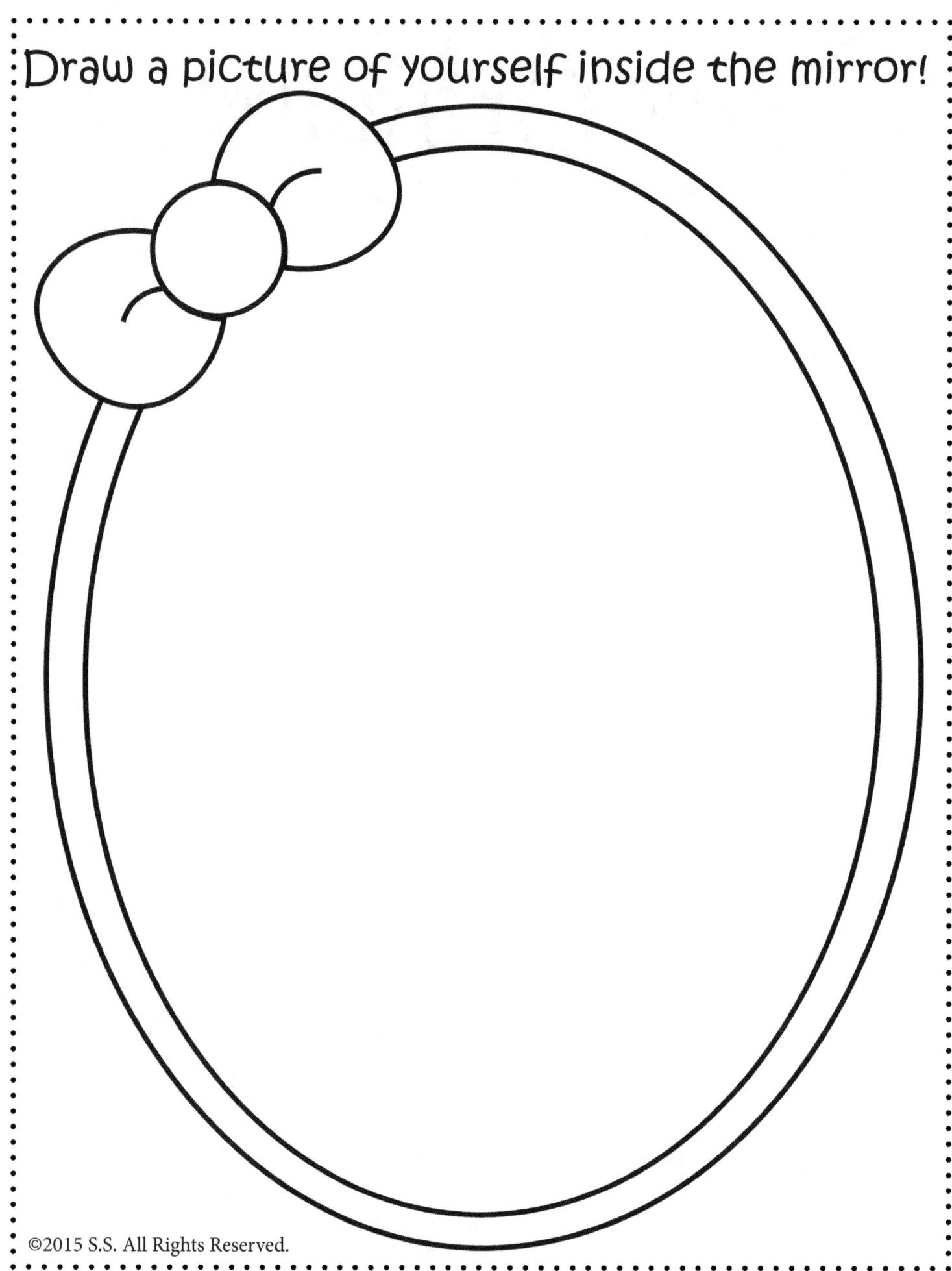

Rainy Days

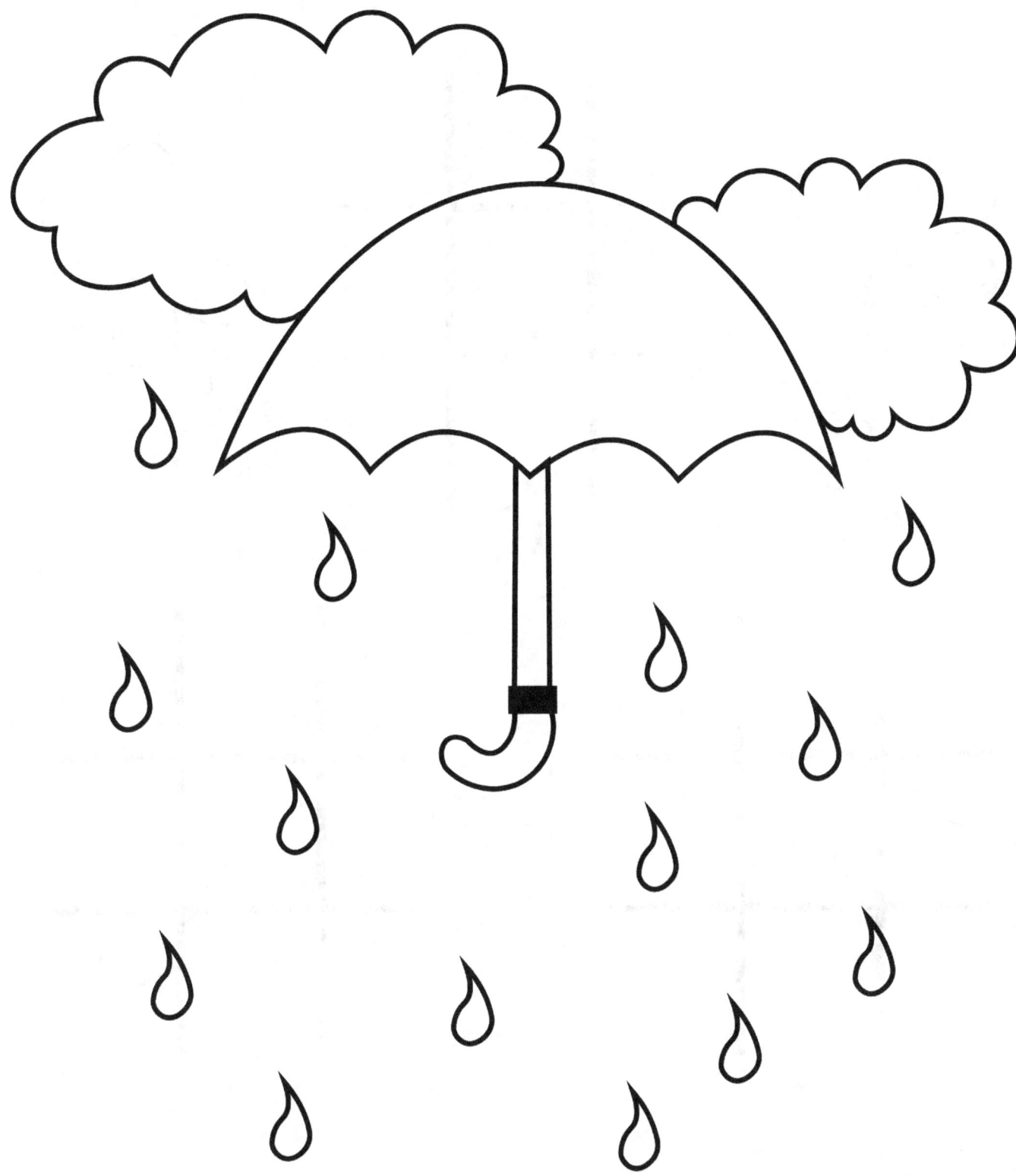

Tic Tac Toe

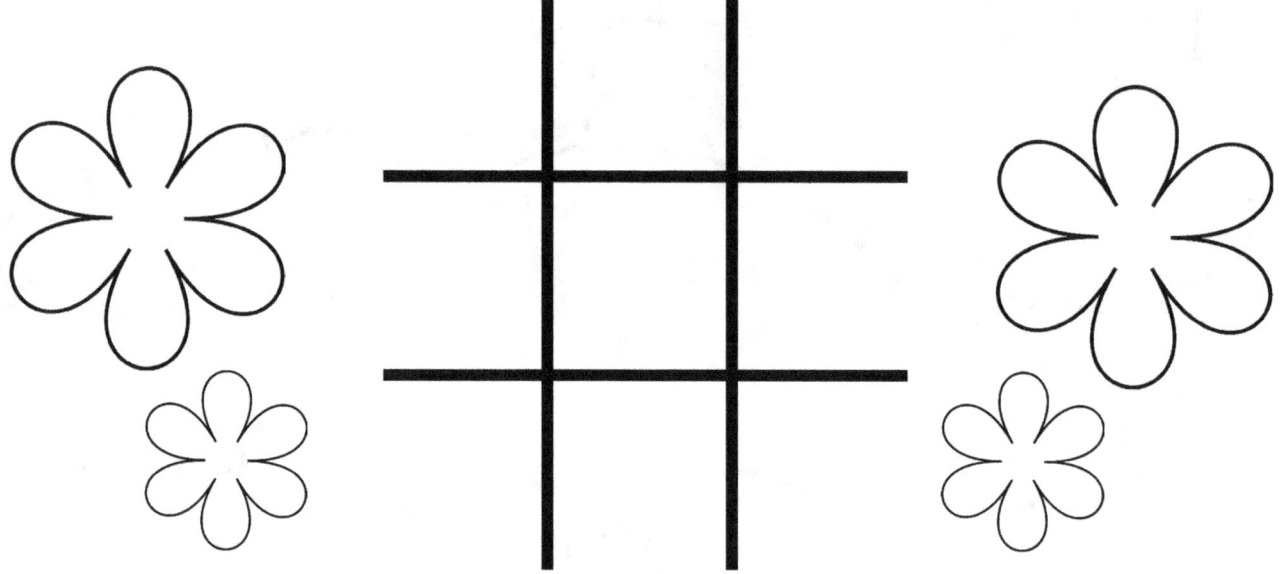

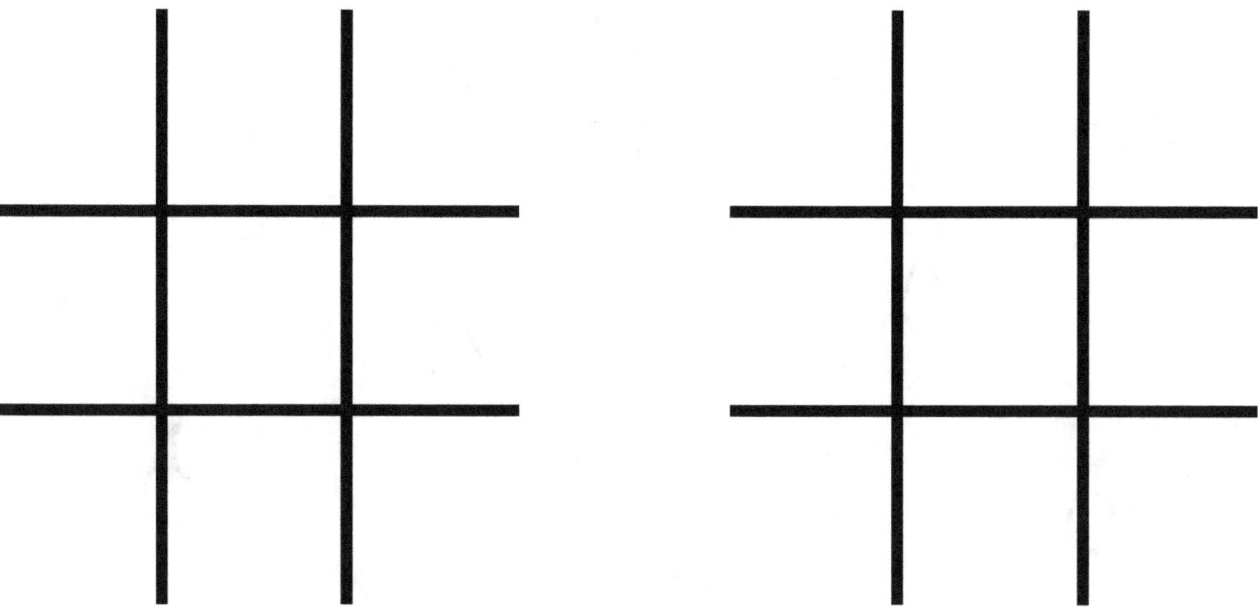

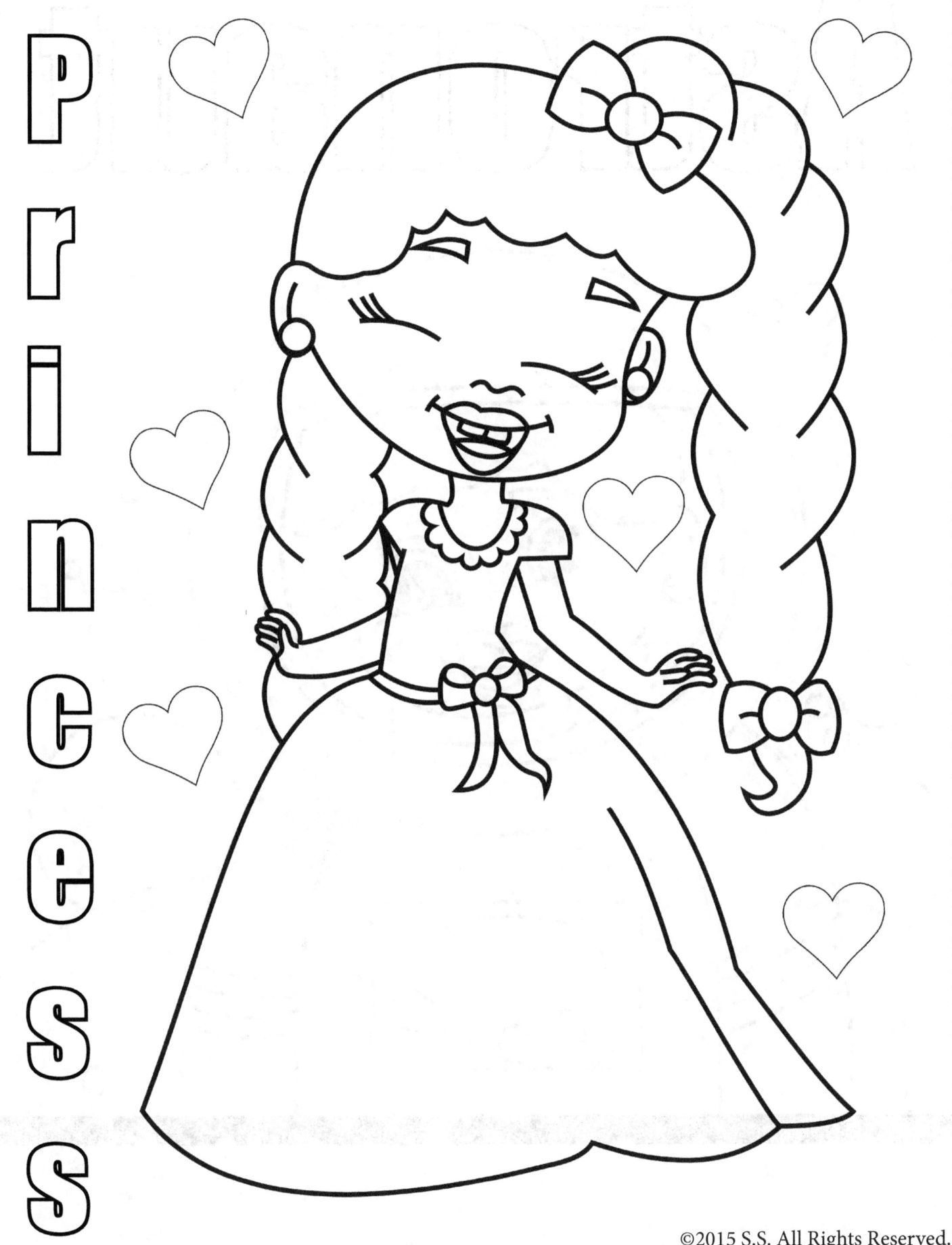

Princess

Astronaut

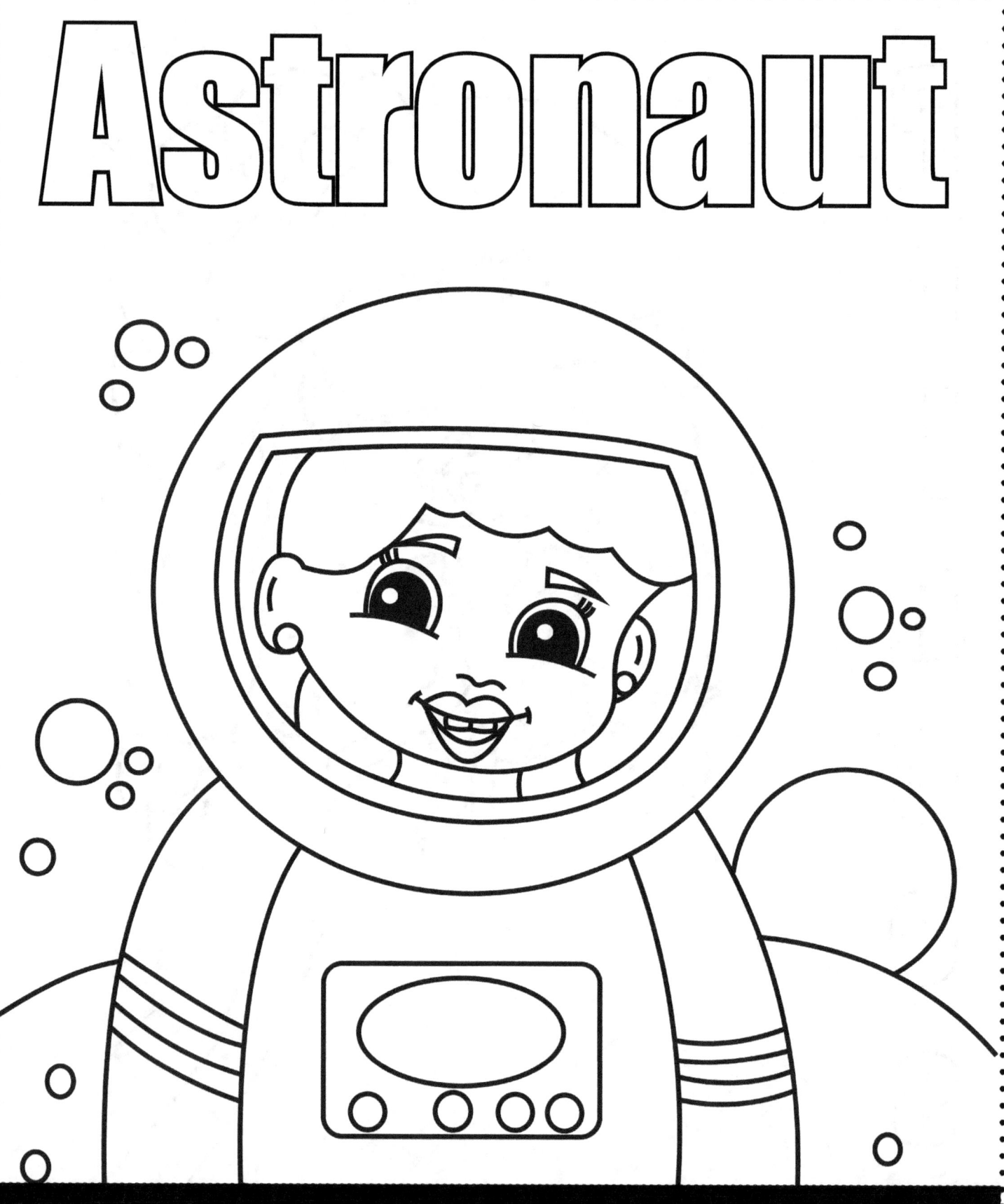

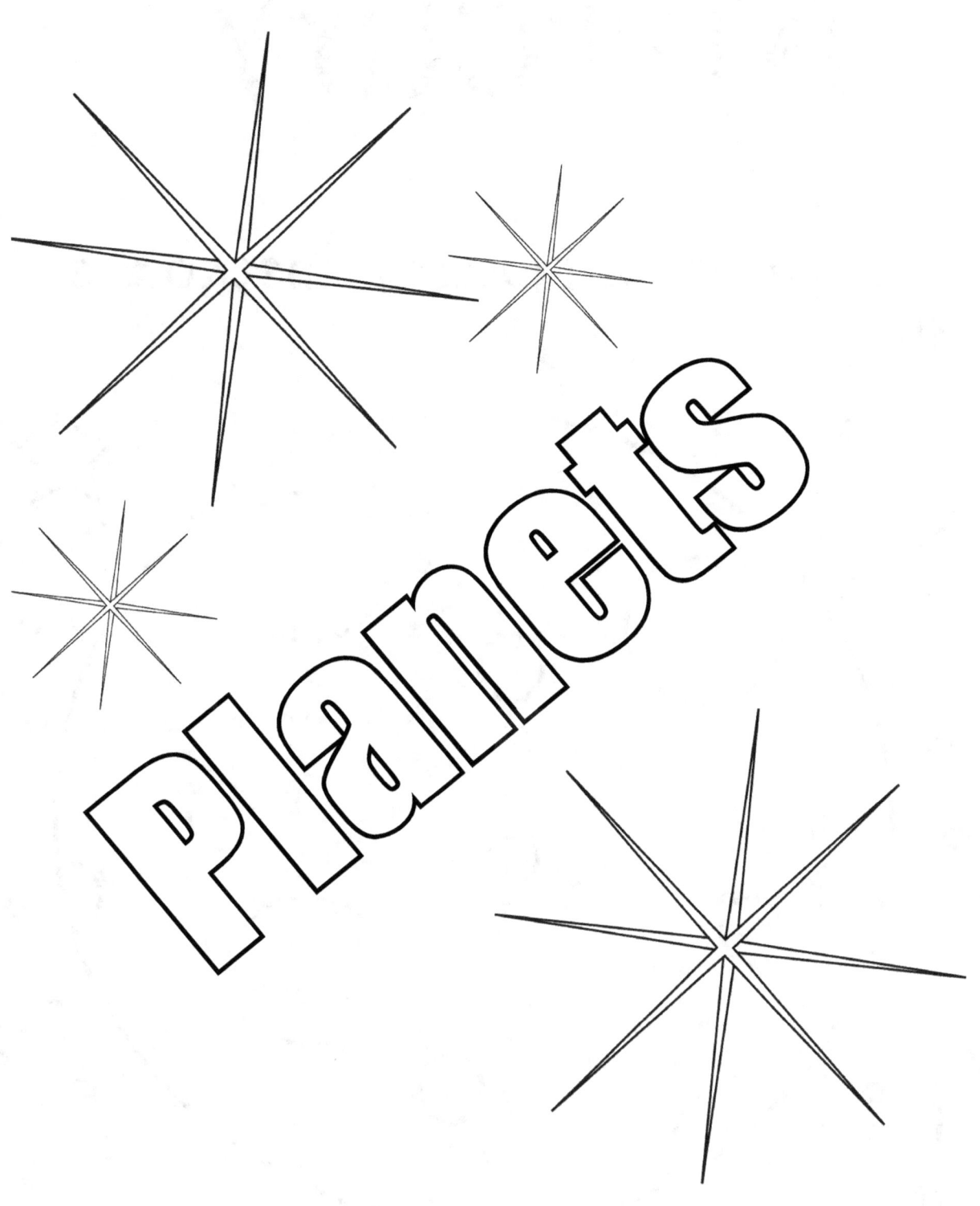

Mercury

Mercury is the closest planet to the sun.

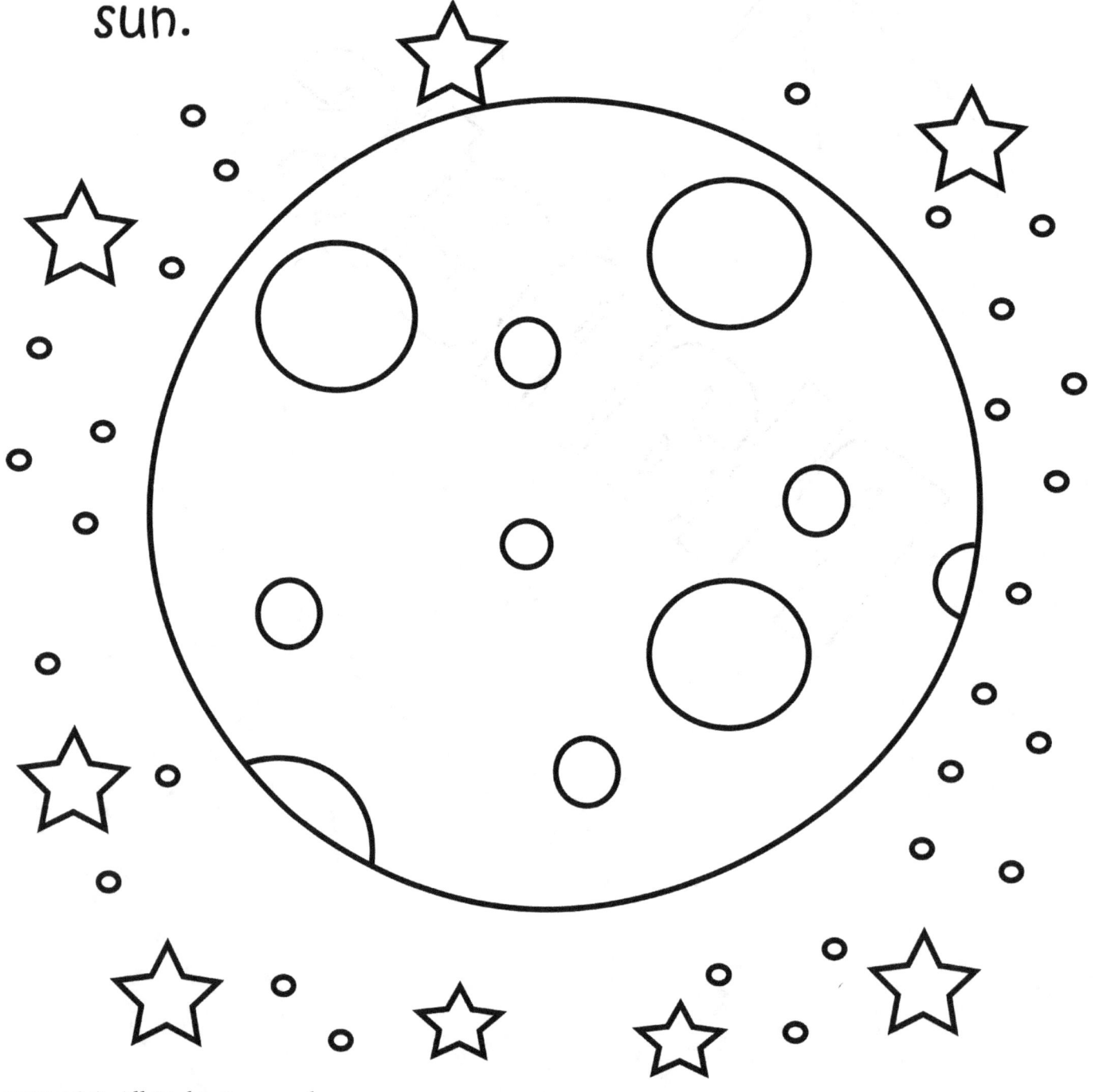

Venus

Venus is the second closest planet to the sun. Venus is the hottest planet in our solar system.

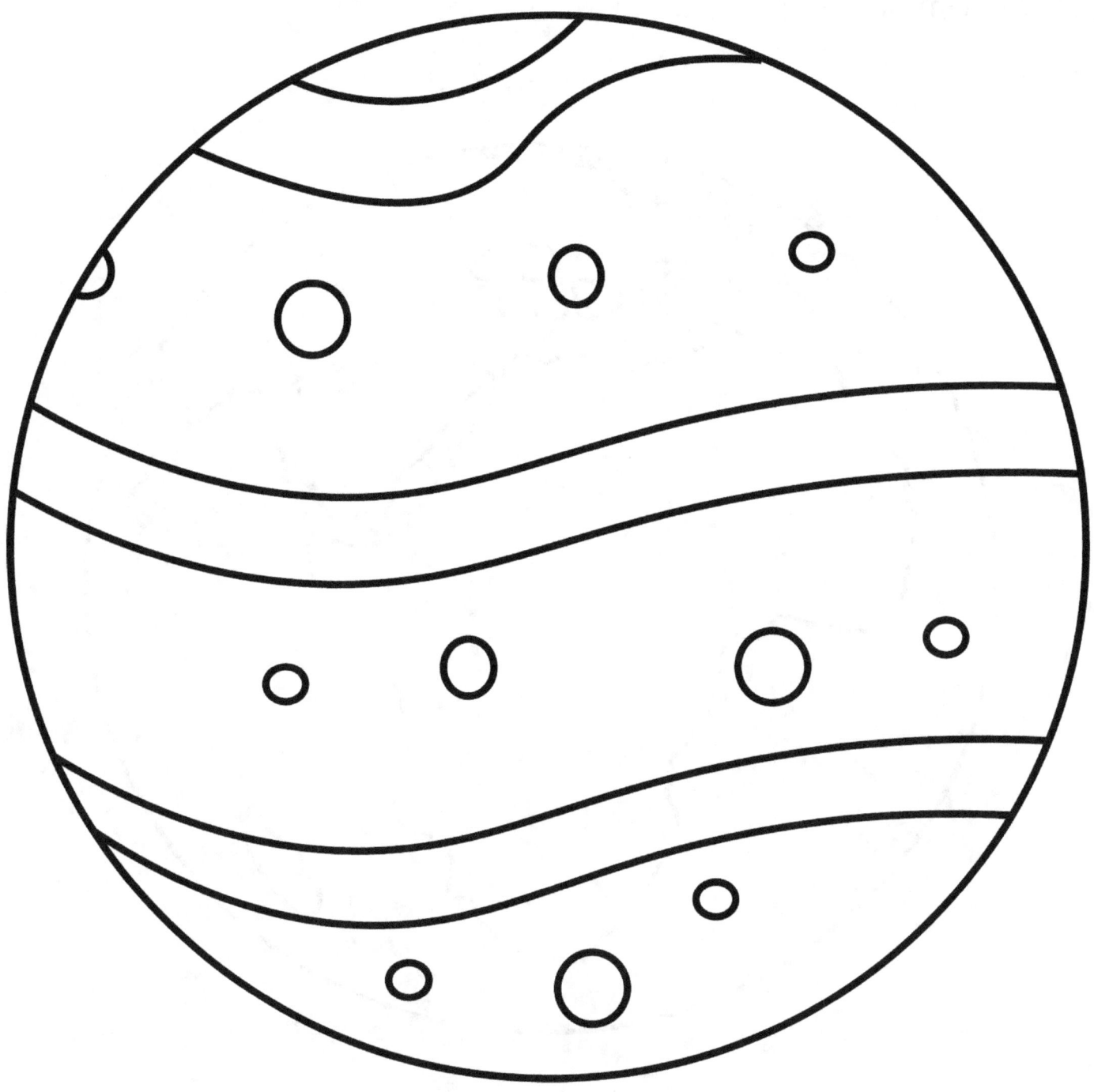

Earth

Earth is the planet that we live on! Earth is the third planet away from the sun.

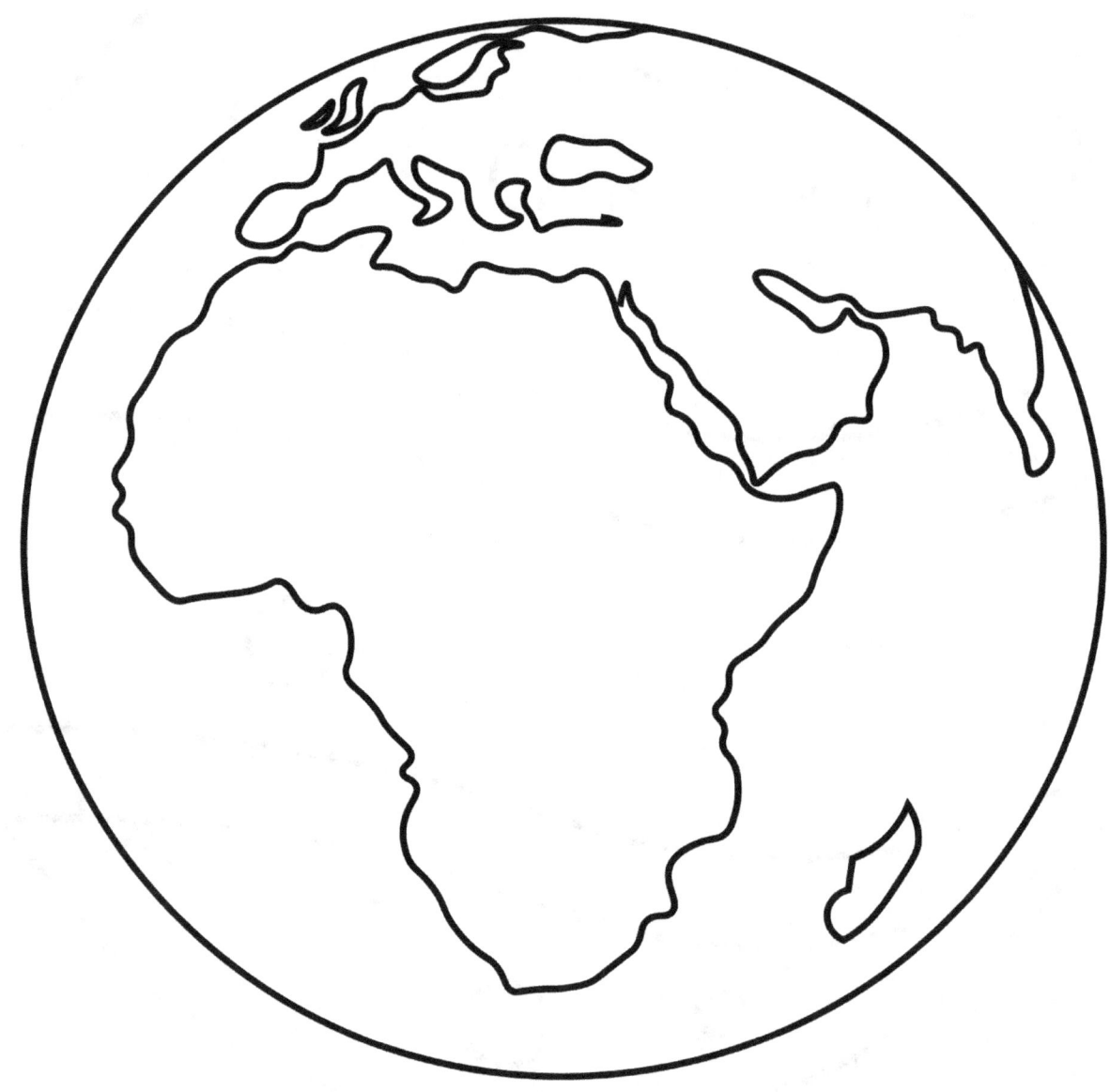

Mars

Mars is the fourth planet from the sun. A nickname for Mars is the "Red Planet" because it looks red.

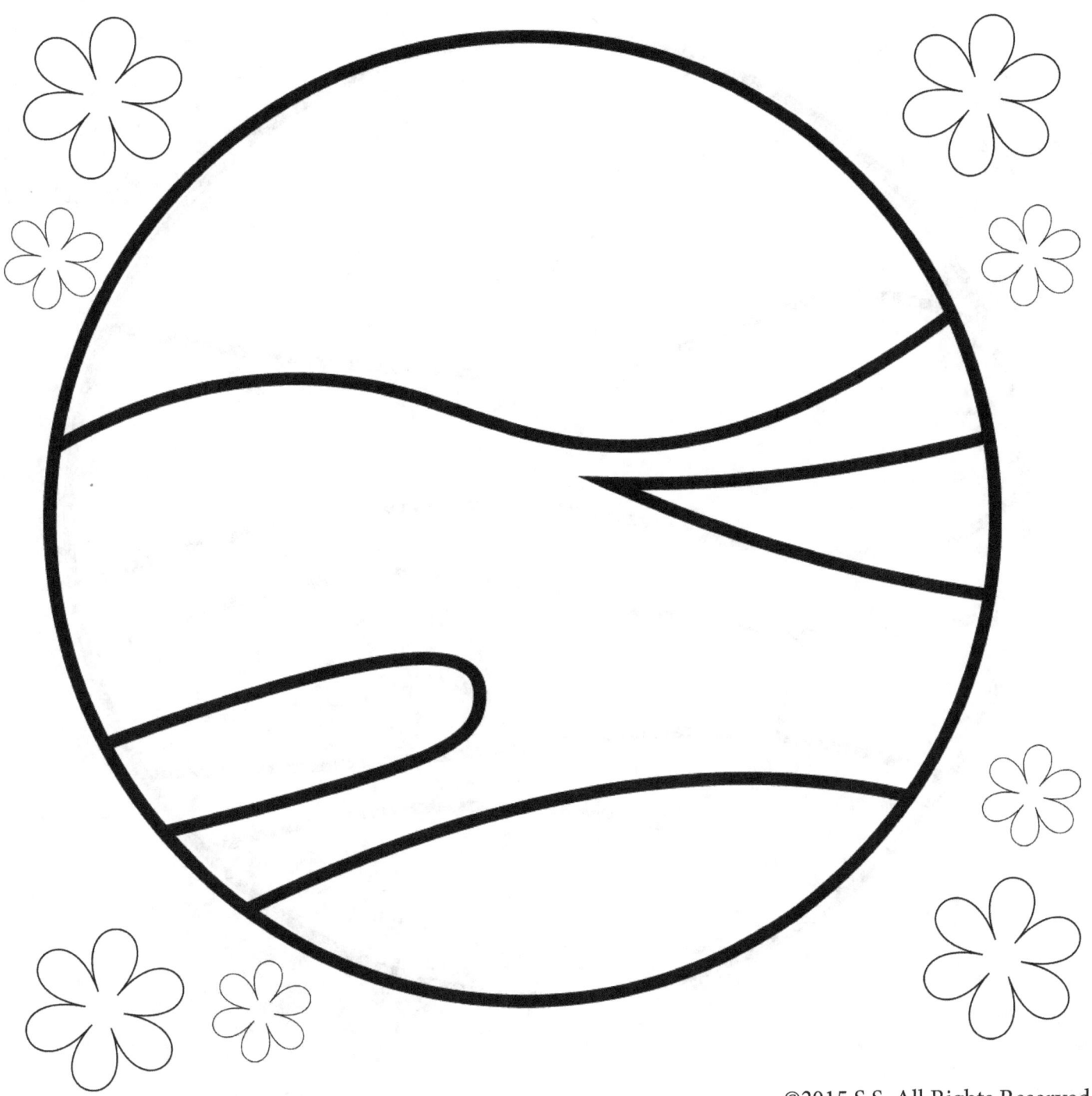

Jupiter

Jupiter is the fifth planet from the sun. Jupiter has the shortest day of all the planets. One day on Jupiter is only nine hours and fifty- five minutes.

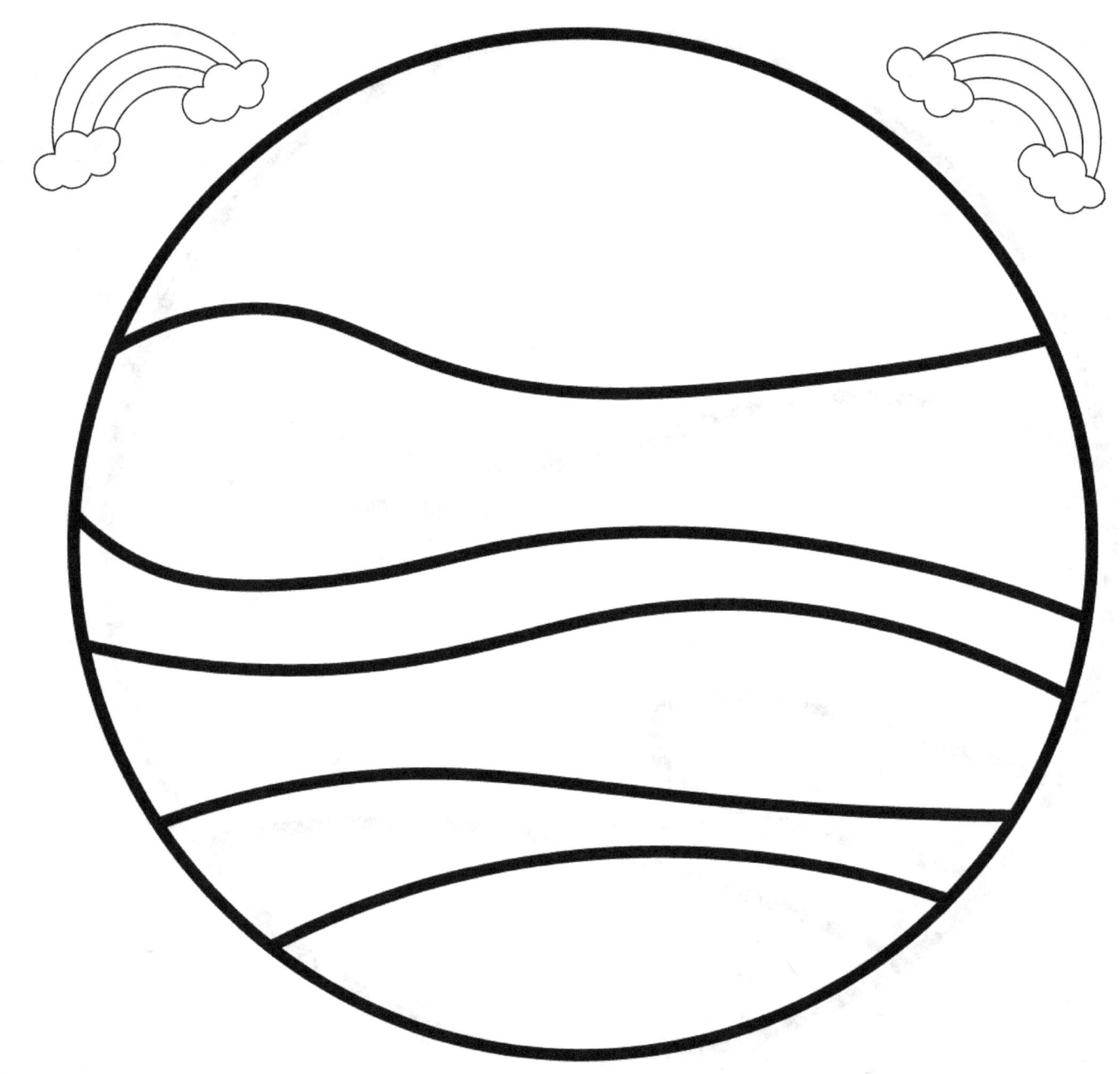

Saturn

Saturn is the sixth planet from the sun. You can see Saturn with a pair of binoculars or a telescope!

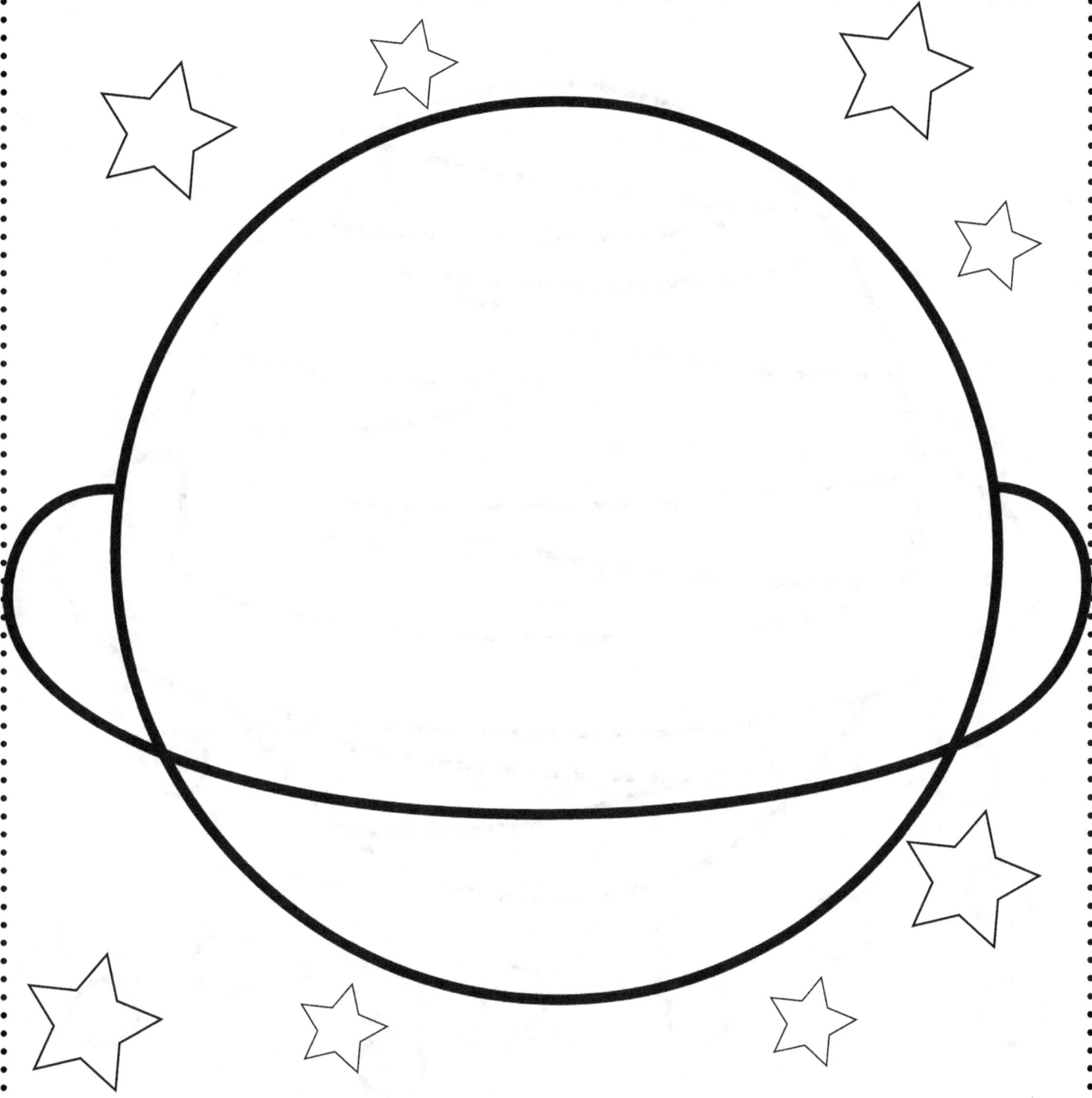

Uranus

Uranus is the seventh planet from the sun. Uranus was the first planet discovered by a telescope.

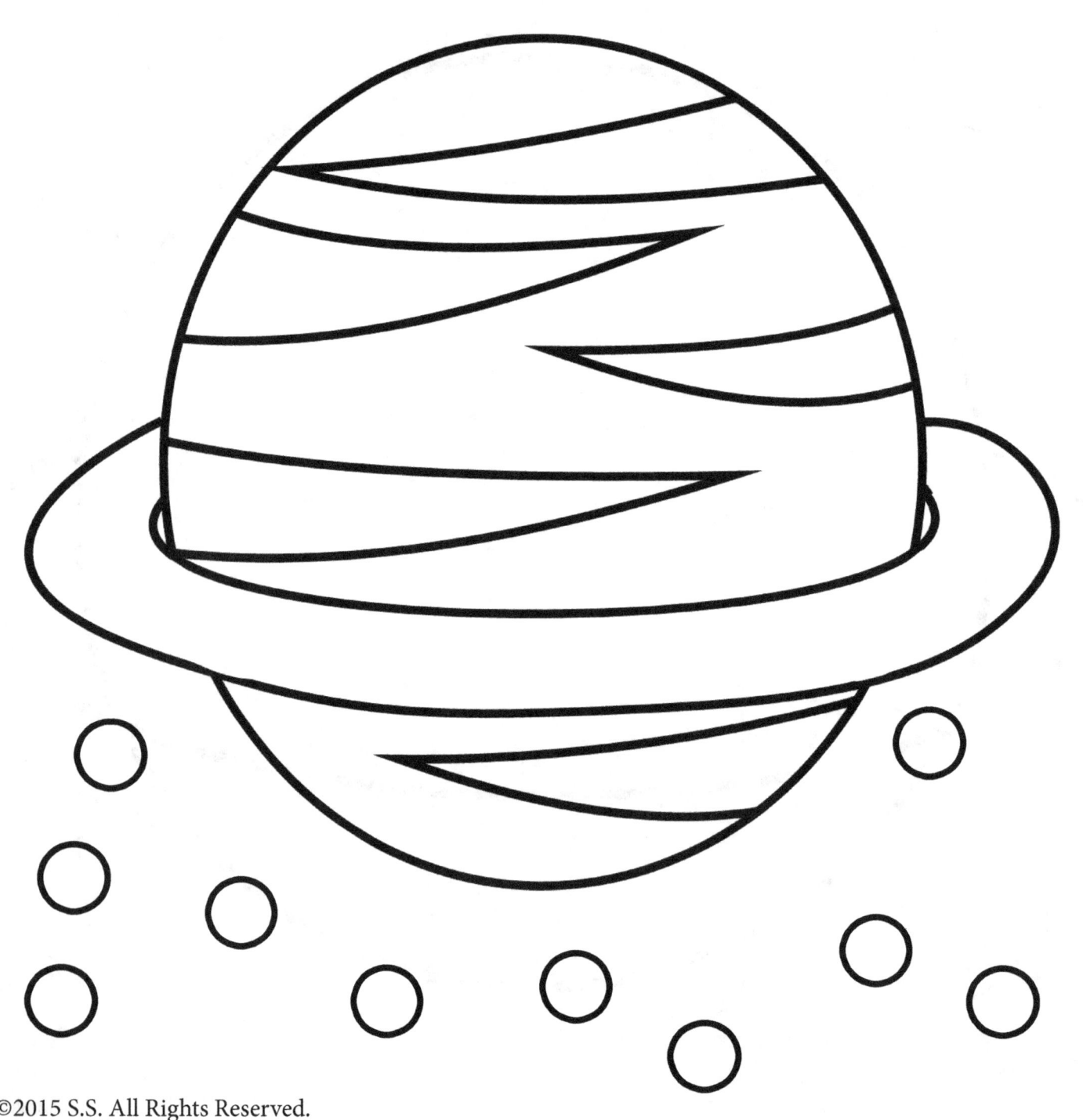

Neptune

Neptune is the eighth planet from the sun. Neptune has fourteen moons.

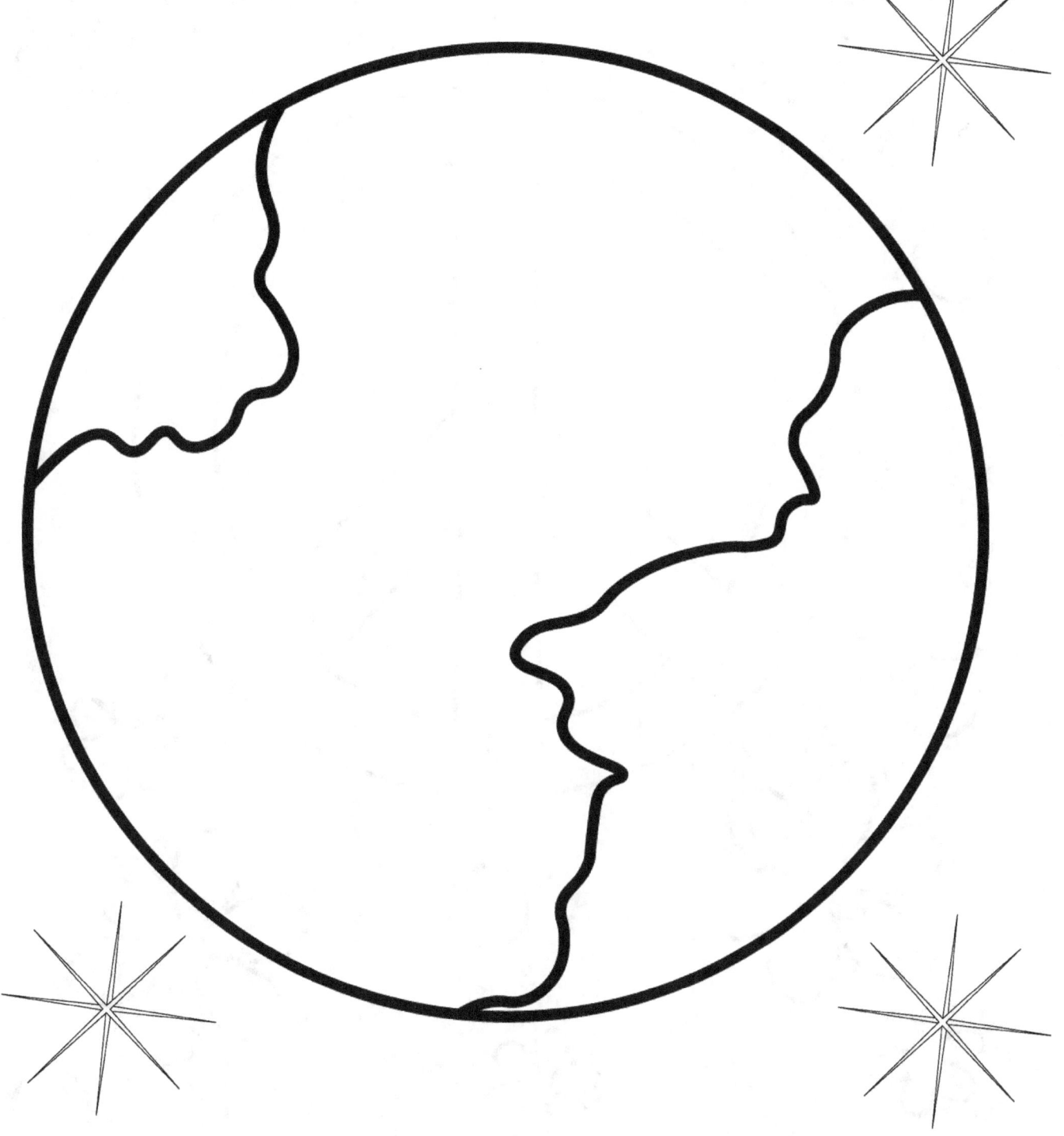

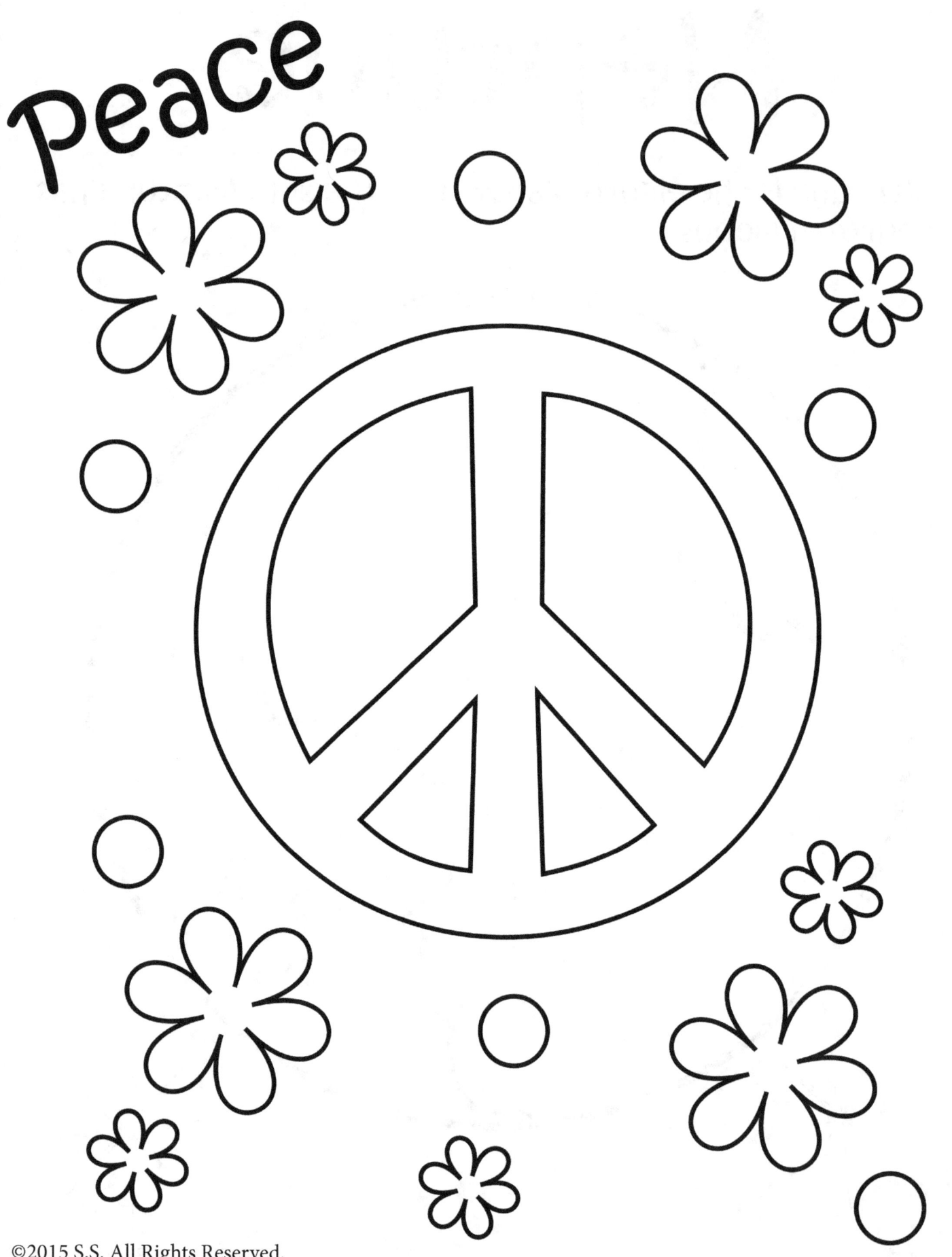

Peace

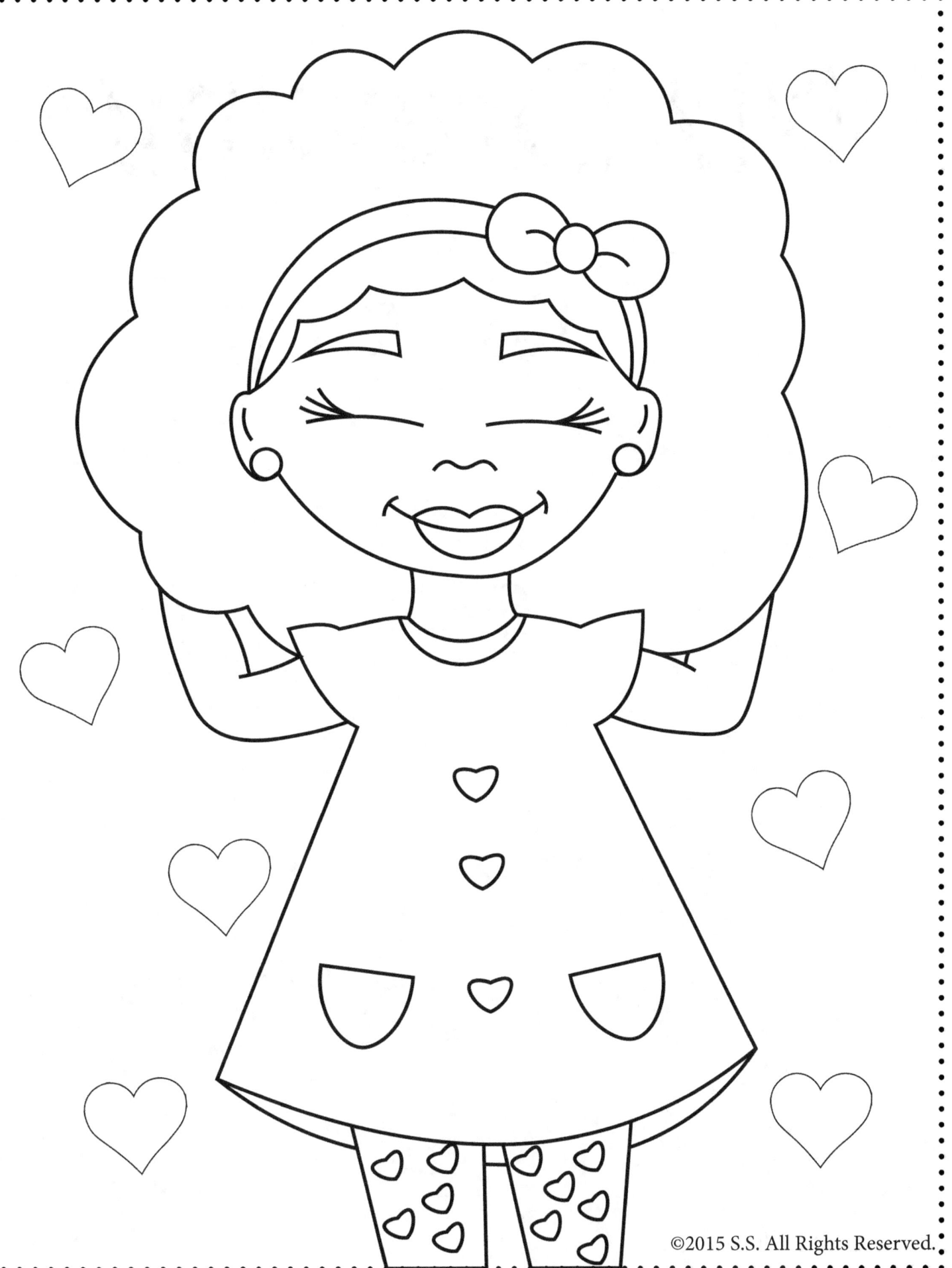

❁My Drawing❁

Smile!

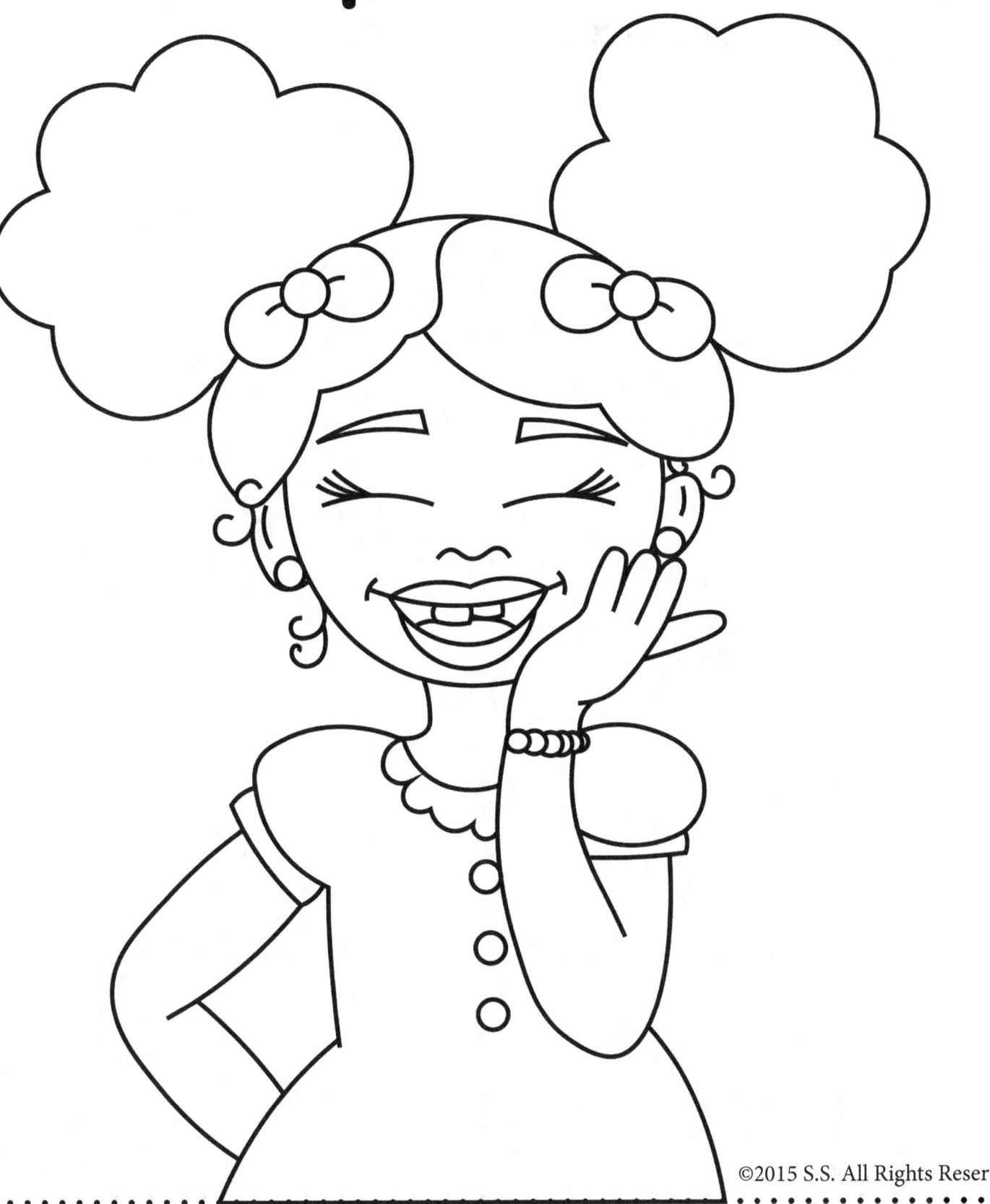

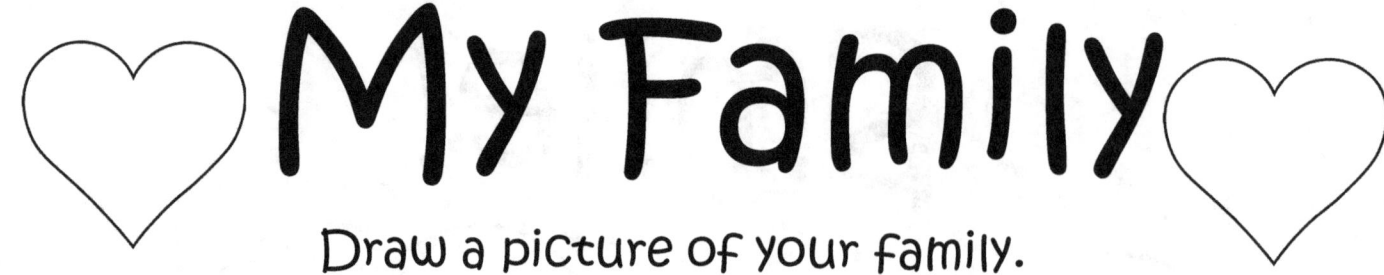

My Family

Draw a picture of your family.

Tic Tac Toe

Winter Ready

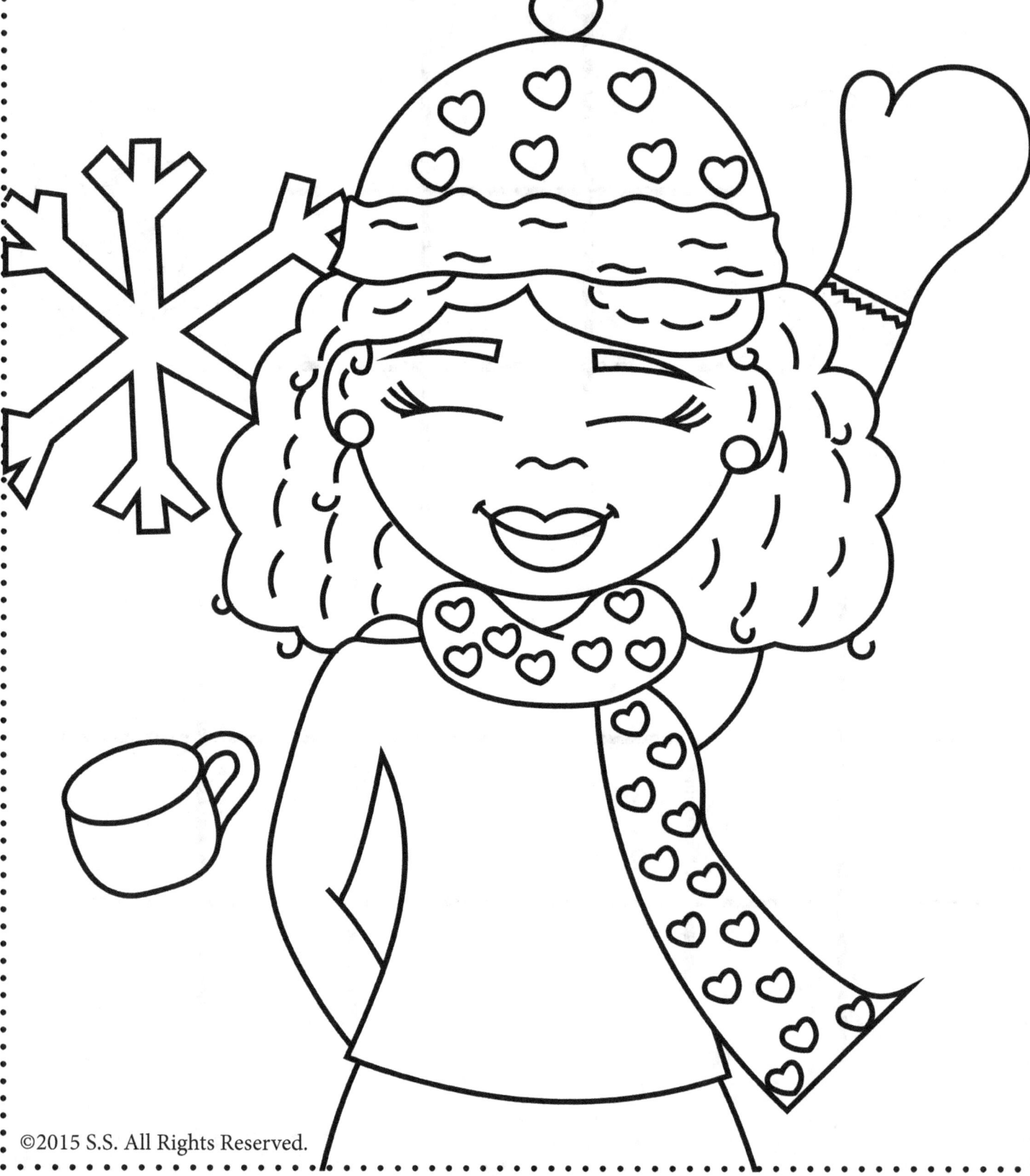

The five senses

Draw a line to match the picture to the right word.

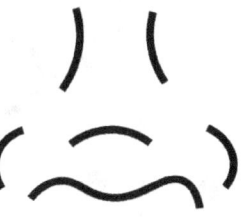 Taste

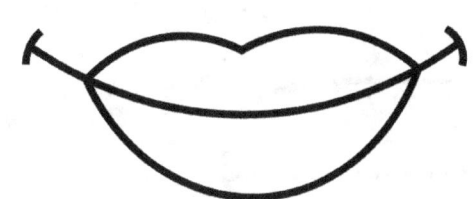 See

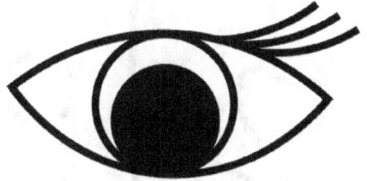 Touch

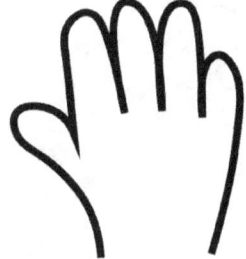 Hear

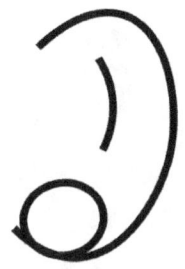 Smell

Camera

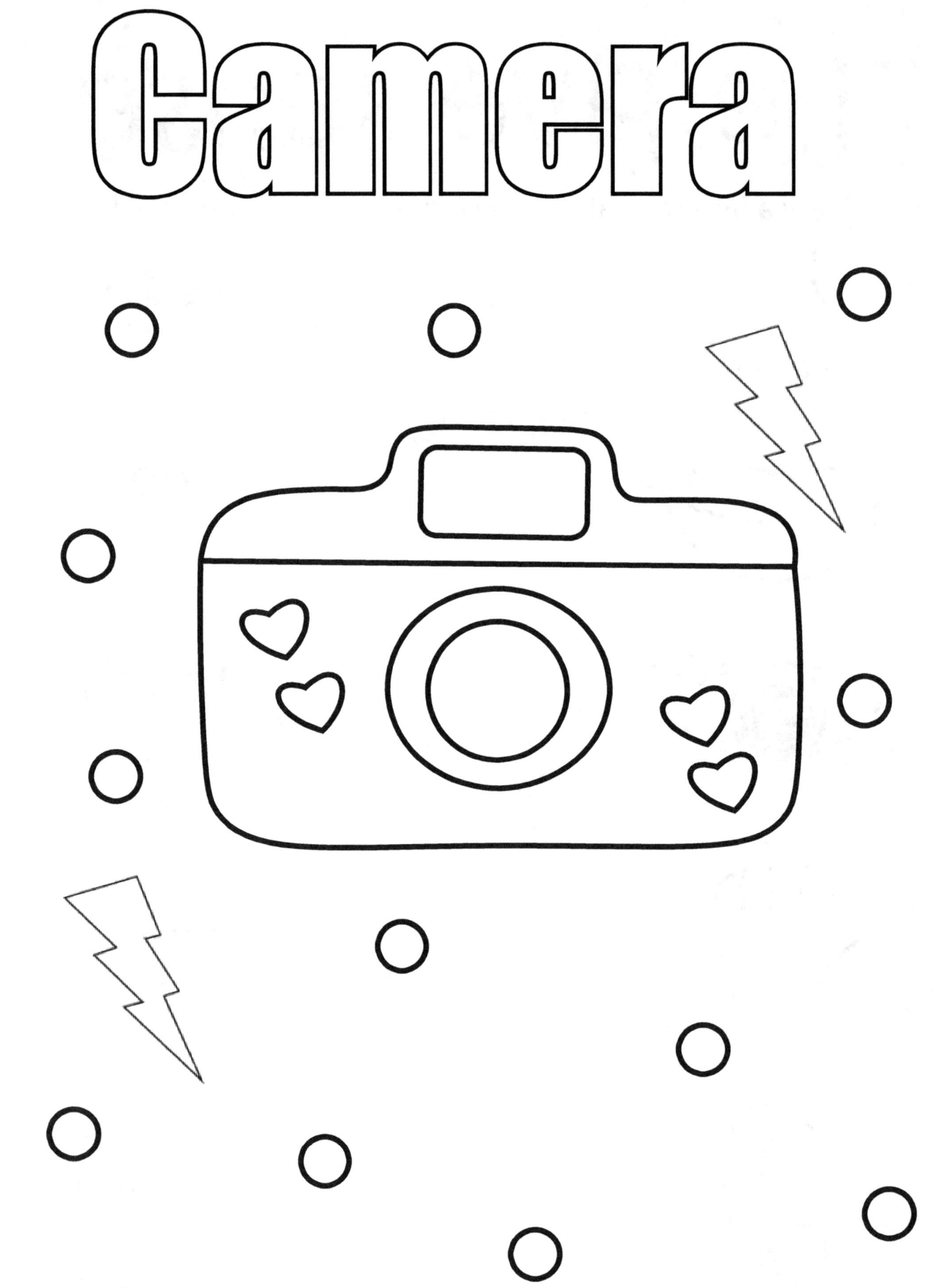

Help the butterfly get to the flowers.

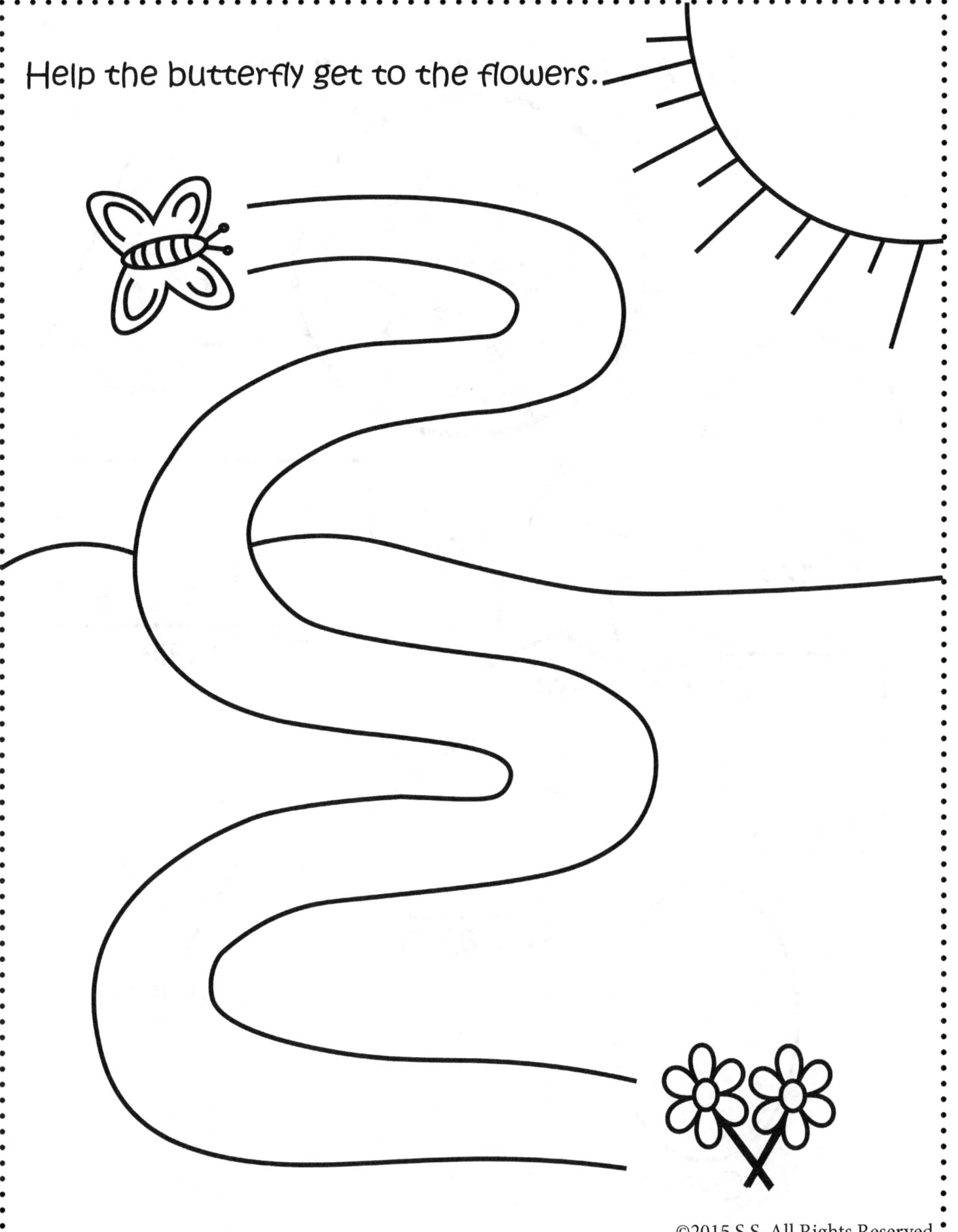

Do you know any of these shapes?

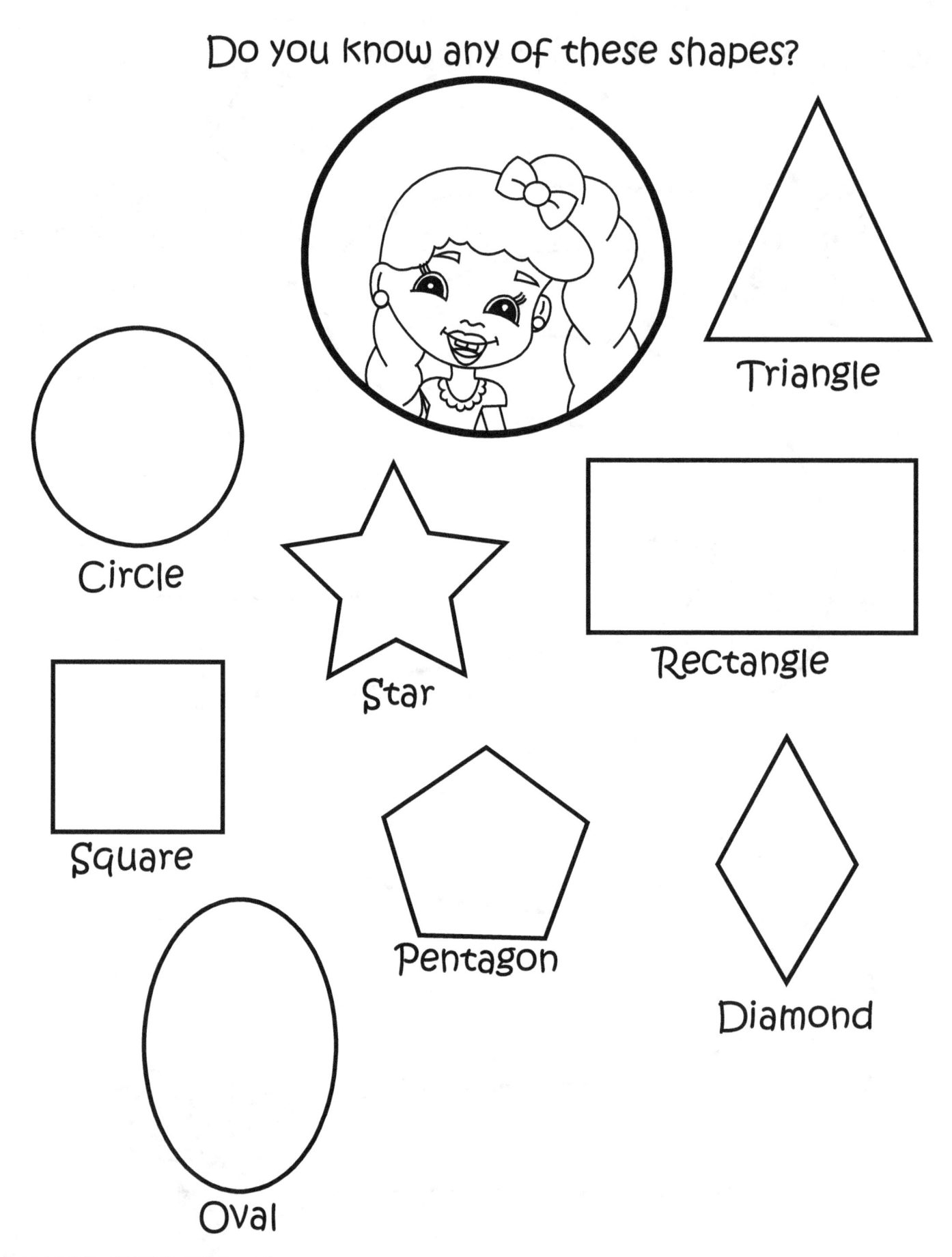

Circle

Triangle

Star

Rectangle

Square

Pentagon

Diamond

Oval

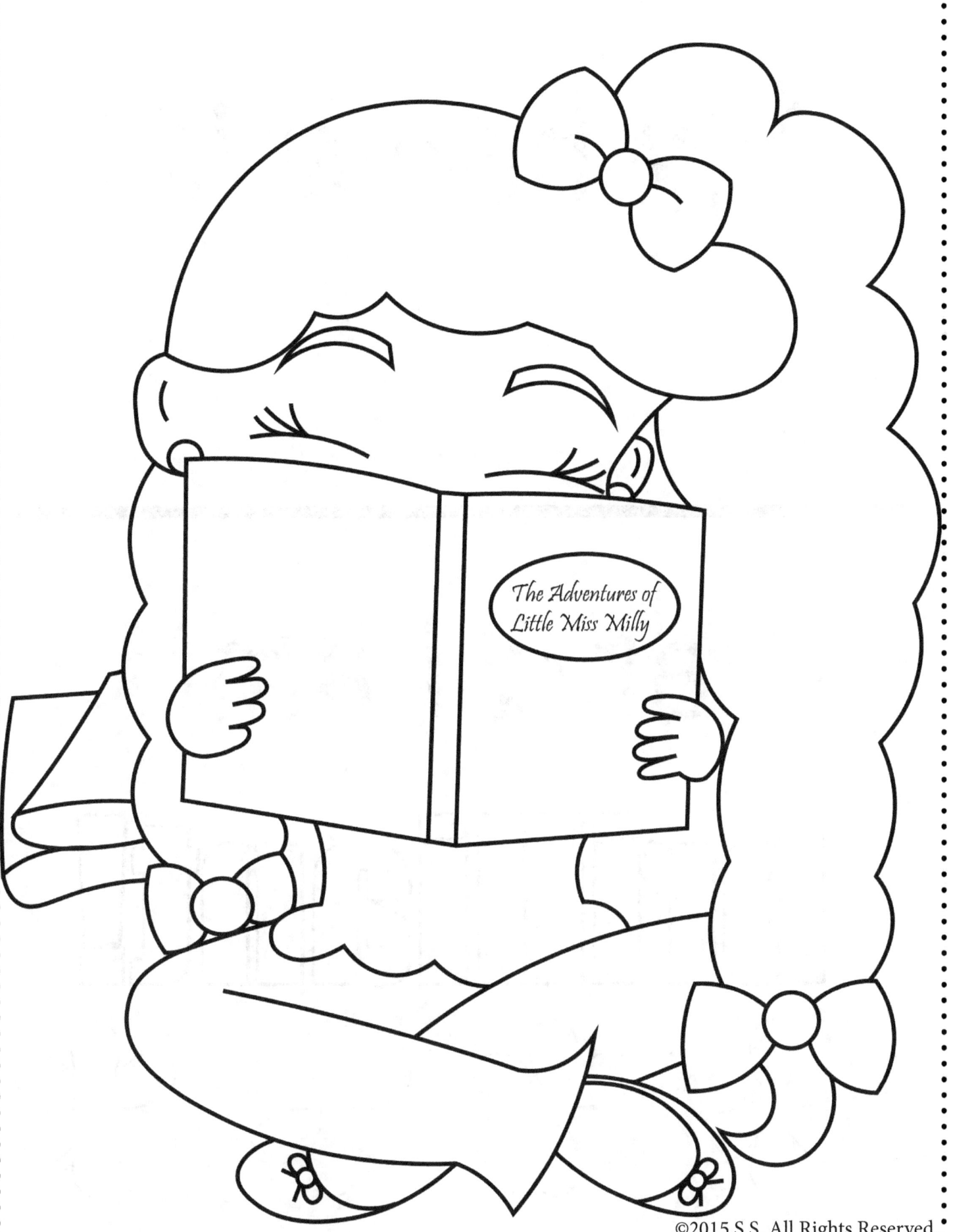

The Adventures of
Little Miss Milly

My name is

_____

and i am

brilliant!

My name is

---

and i am

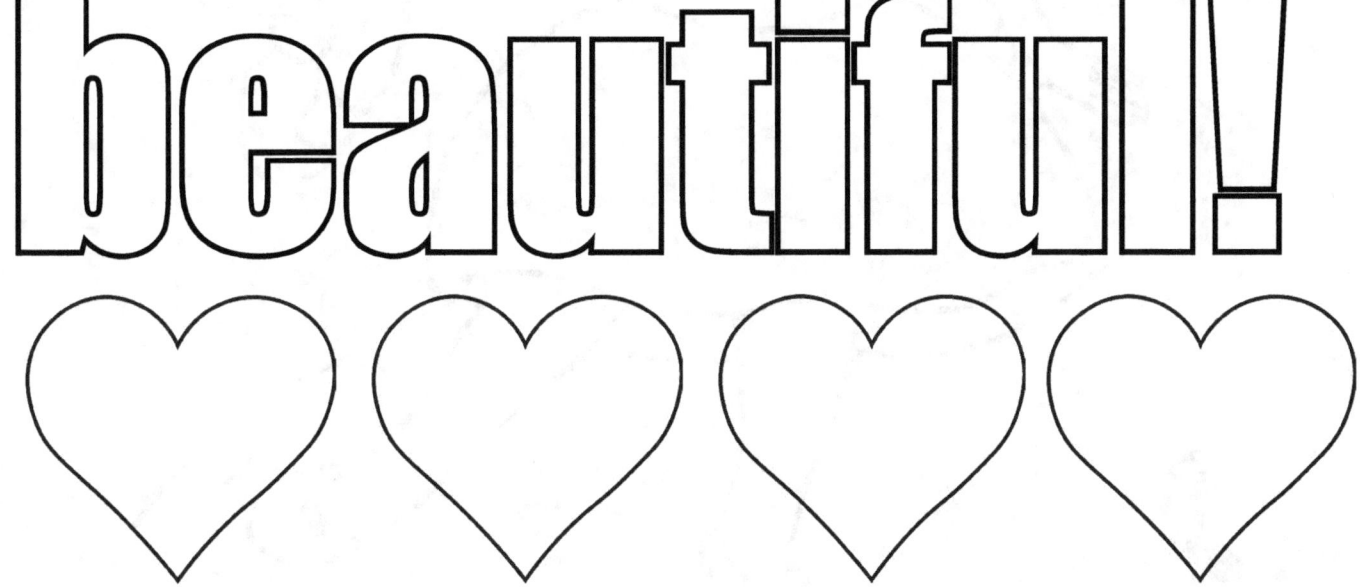

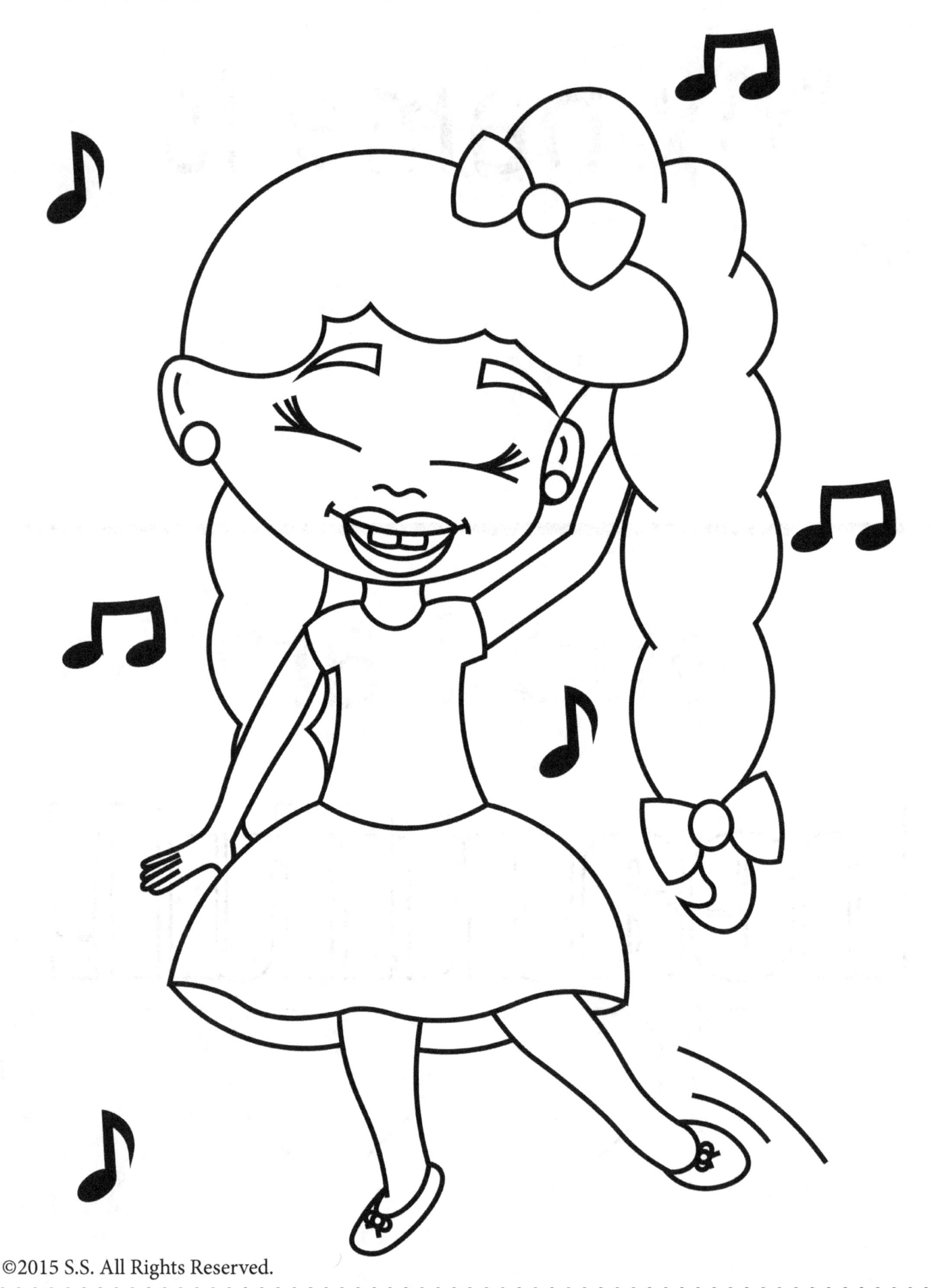

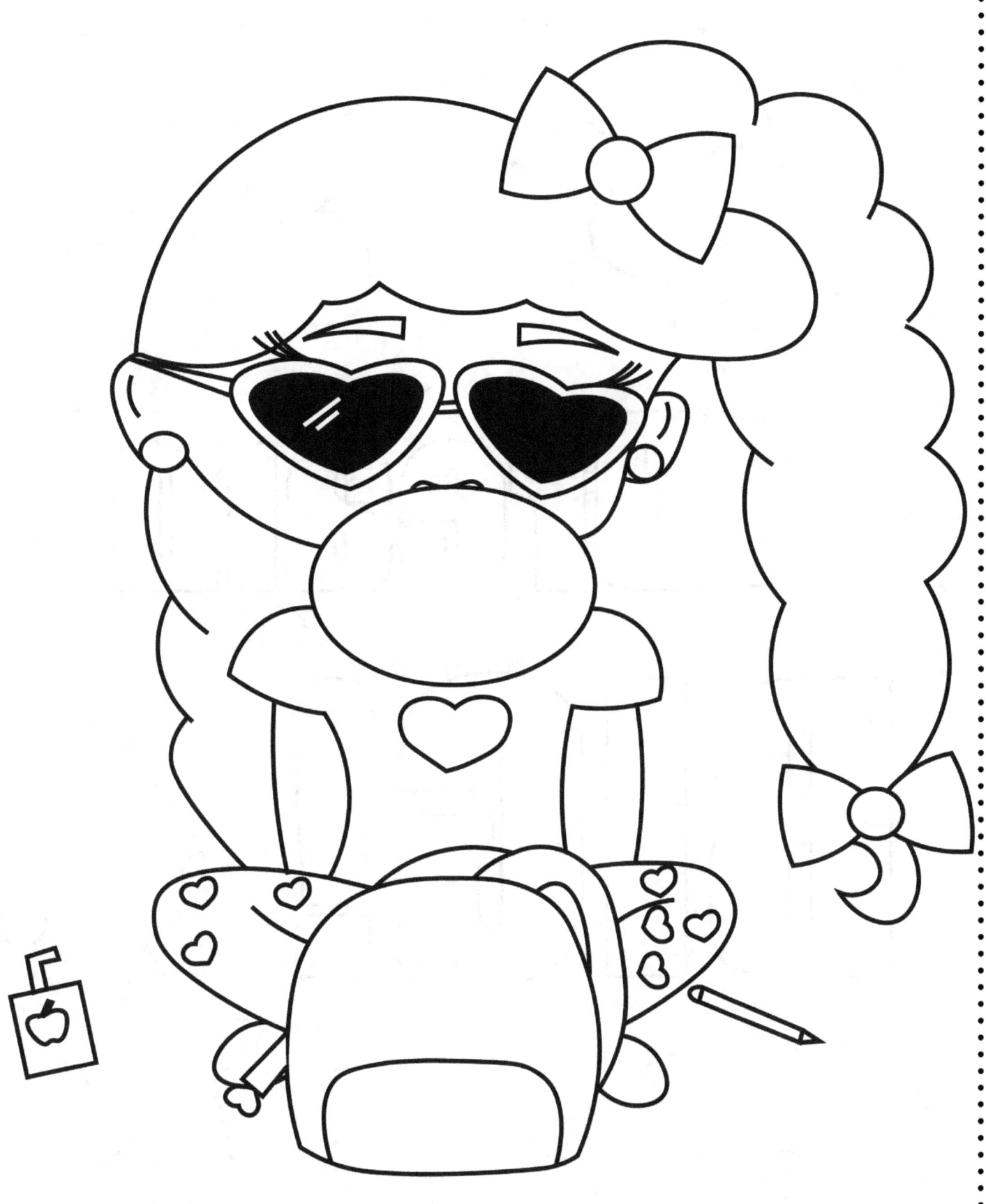

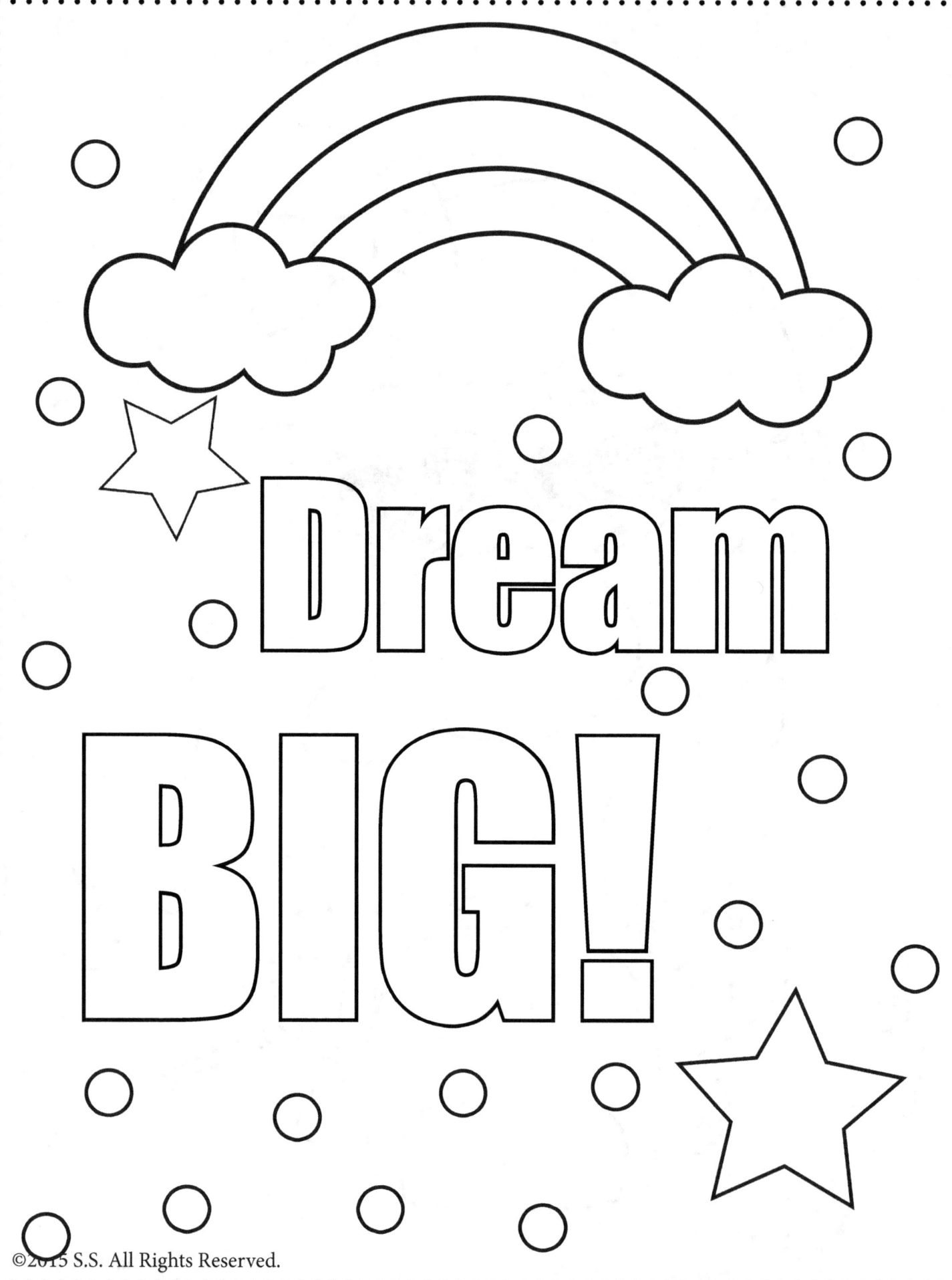

What time is it?

Look at the clocks below and write what time it is.

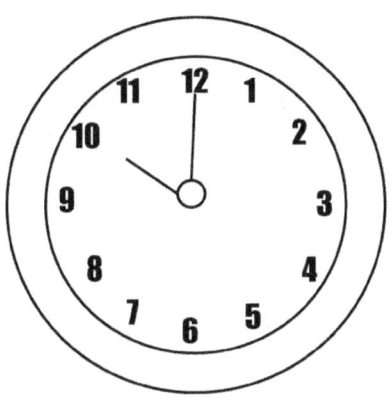

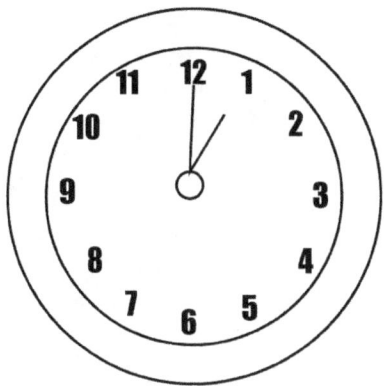

_____

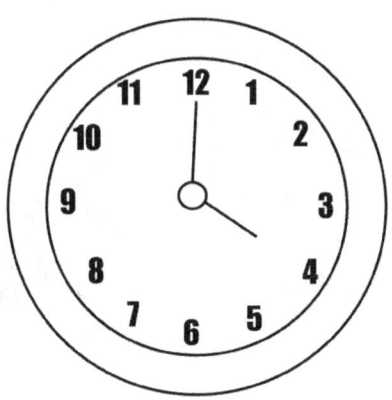

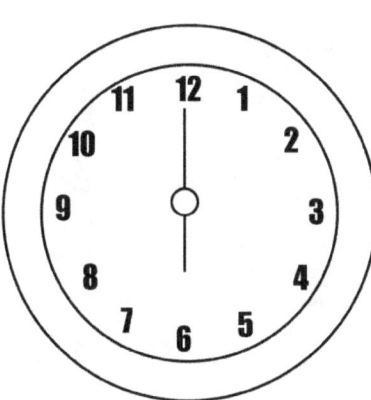

_____

Doodle

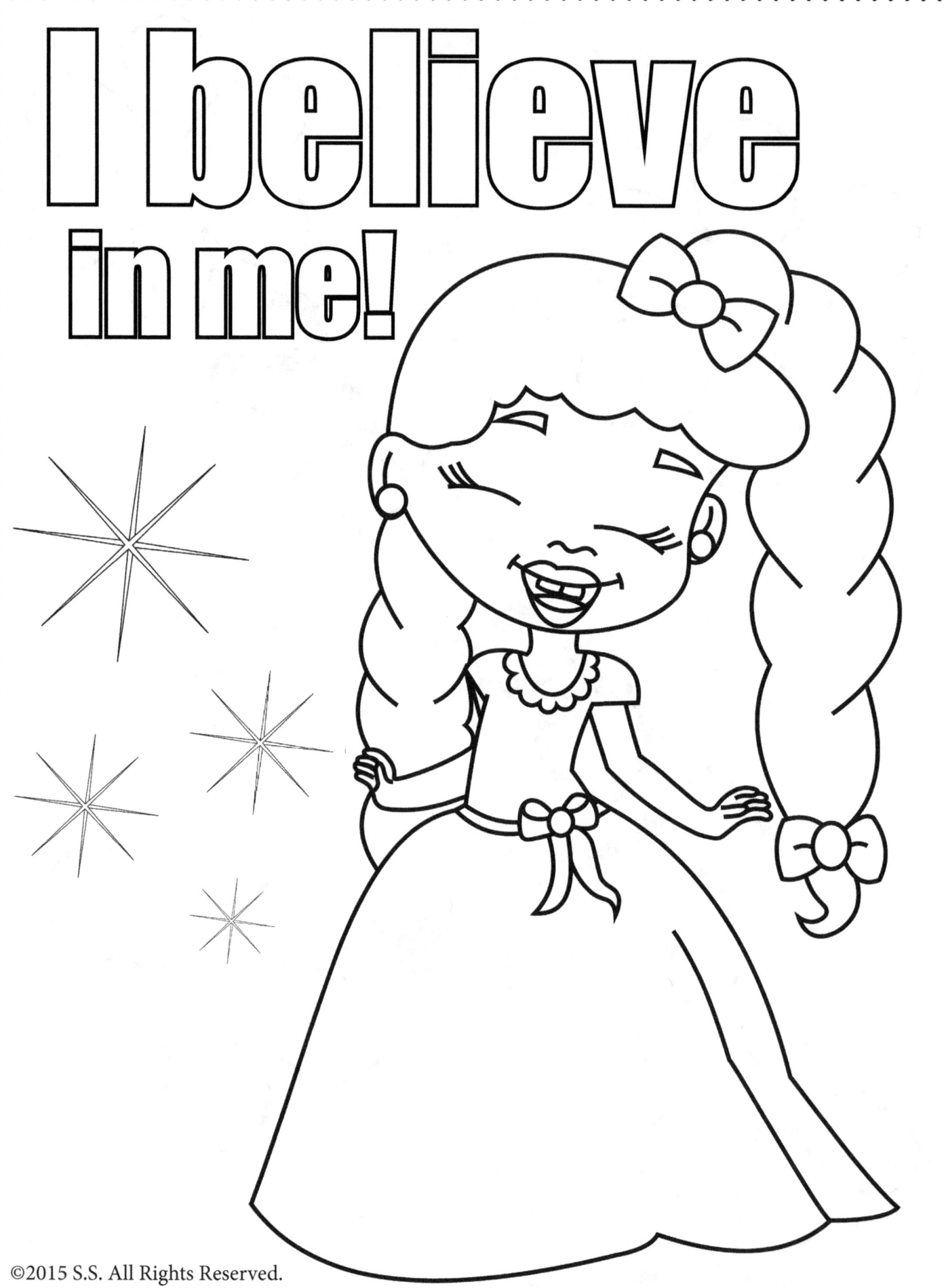

I believe in me!

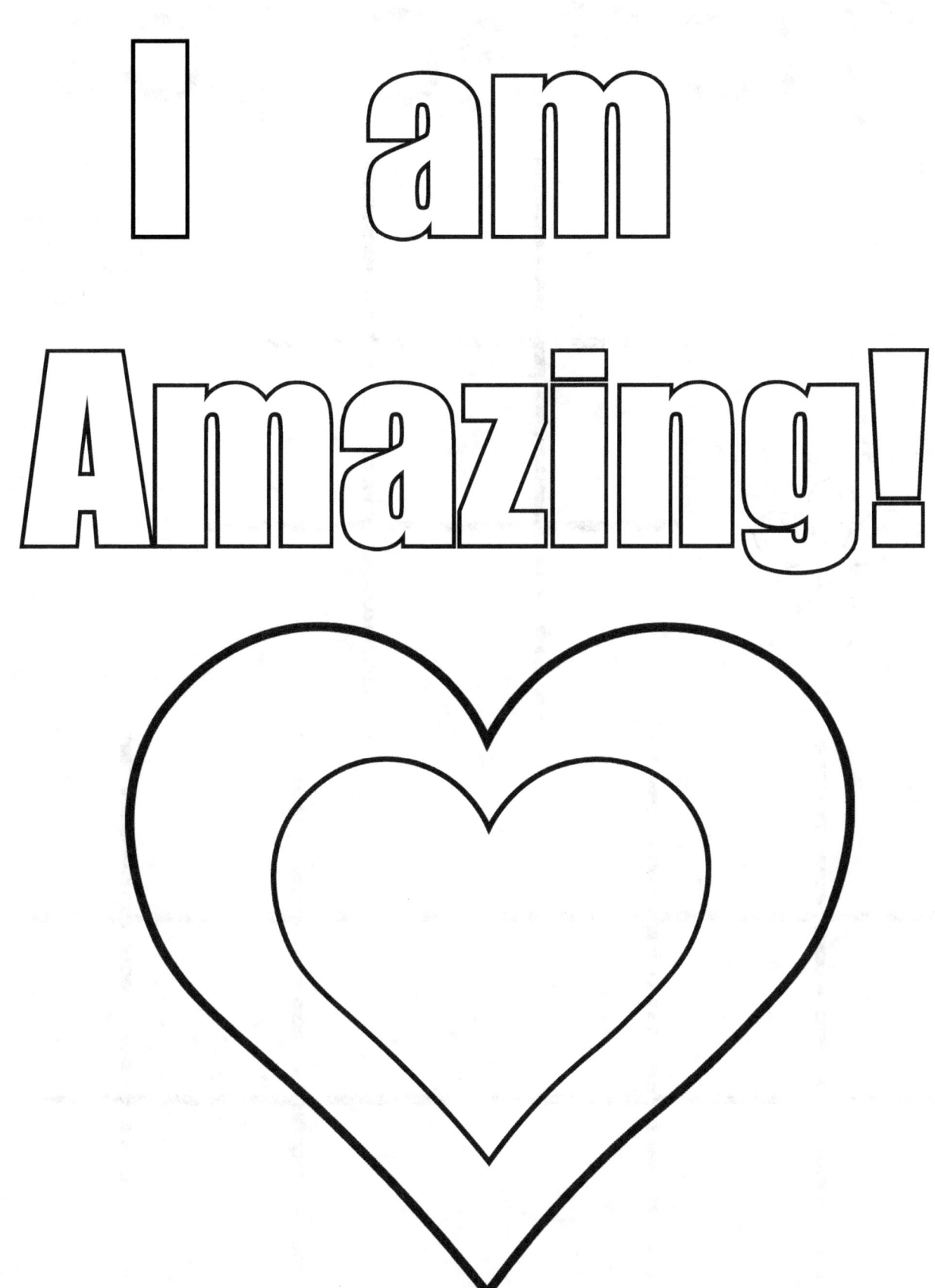

I am Amazing!

Tic Tac Toe

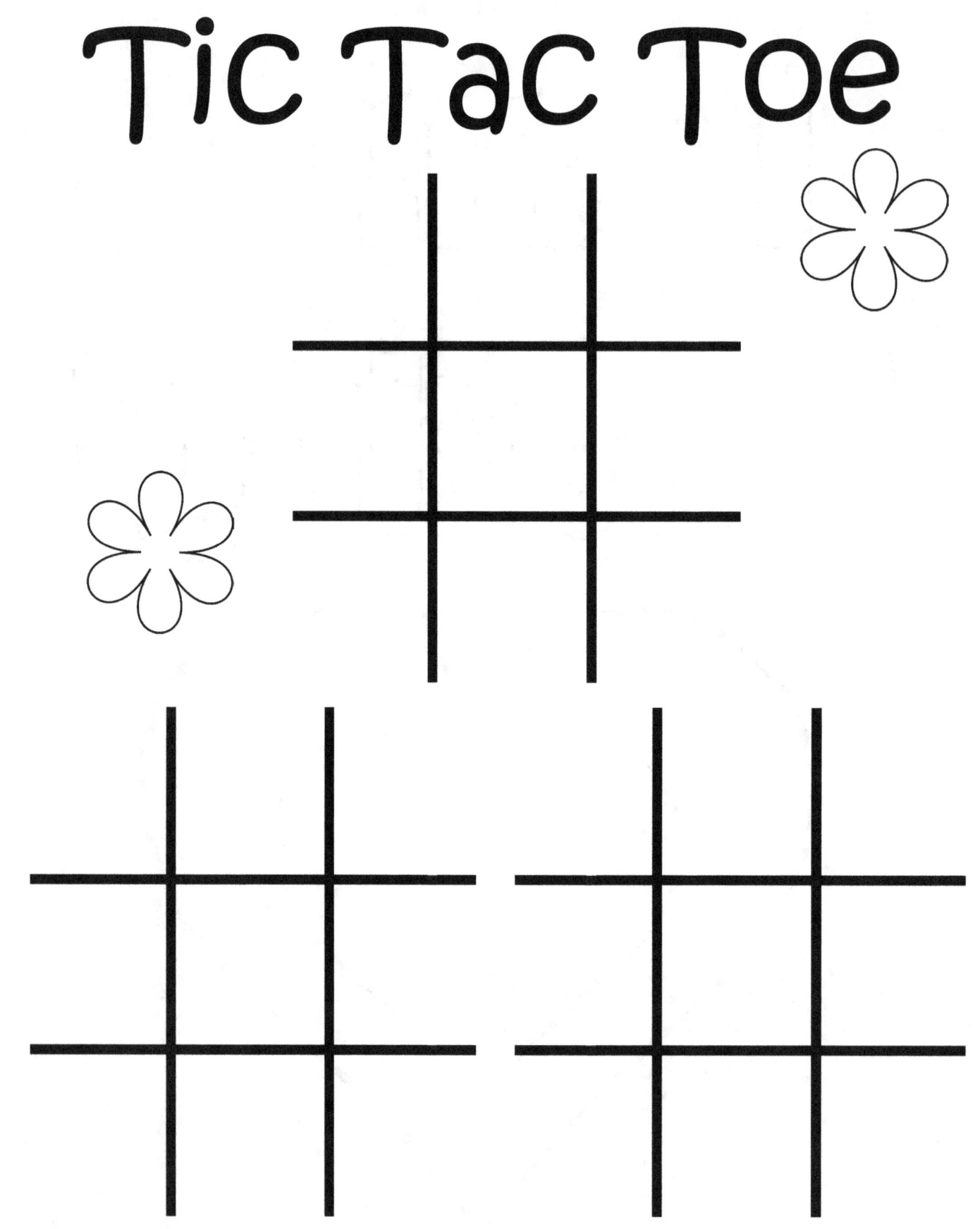

My Drawing

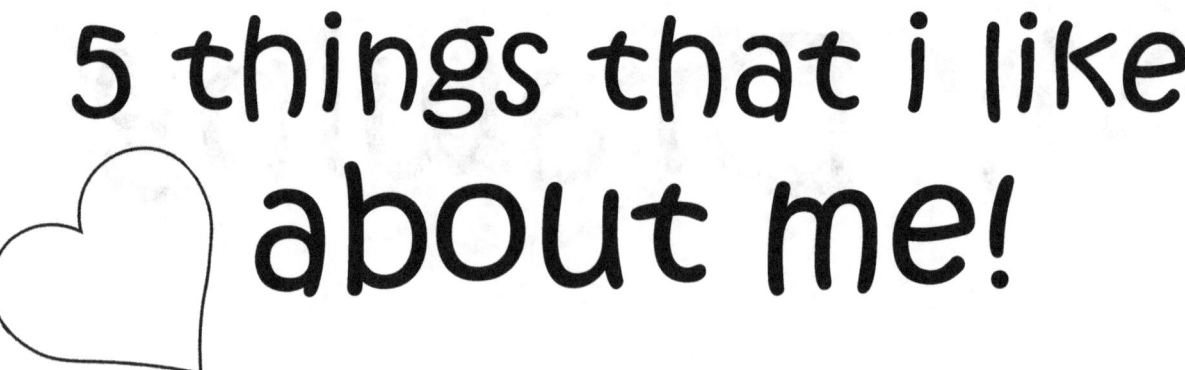

5 things that i like about me!

1. _____

2. _____

3. _____

4. _____

5. _____

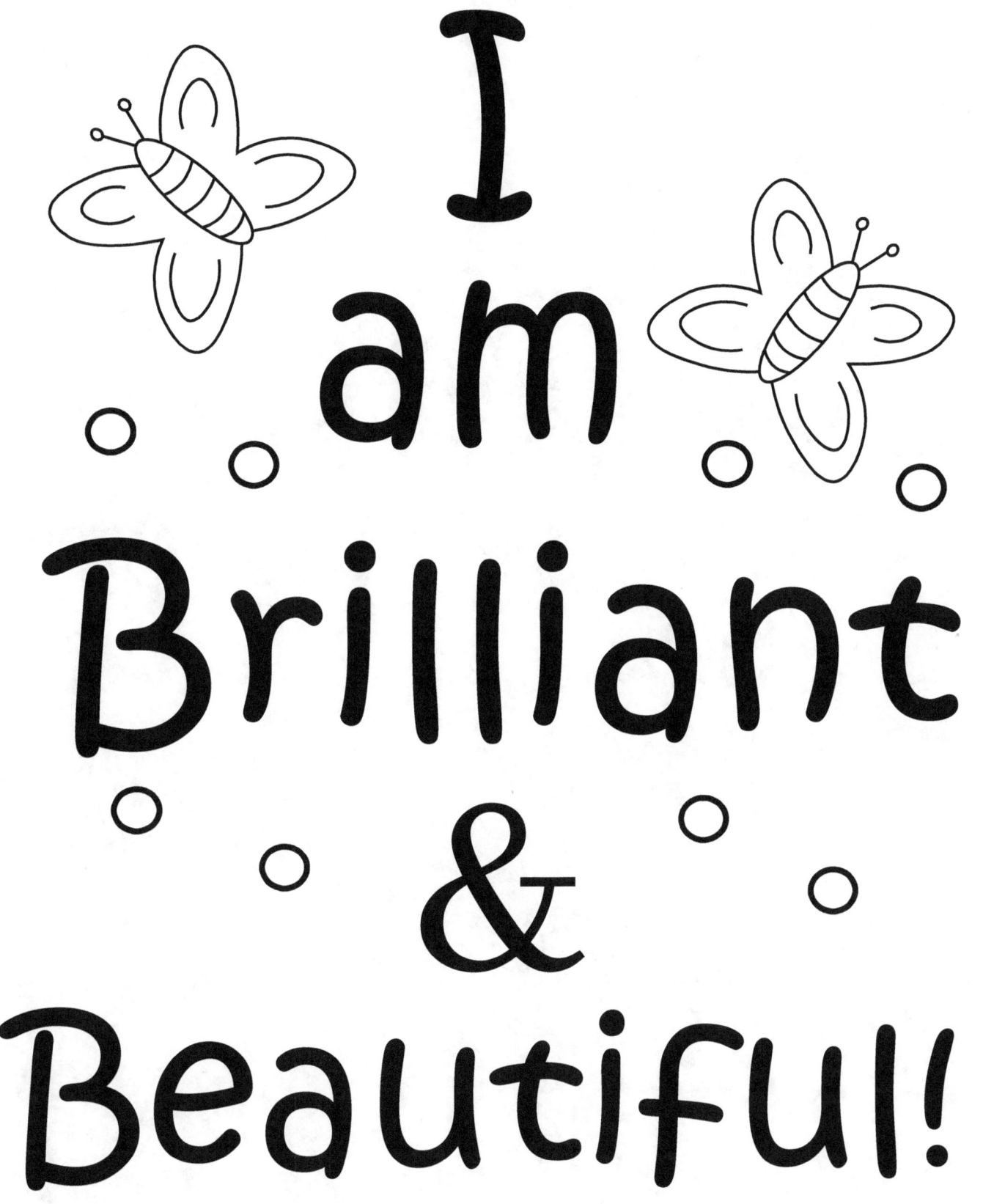

I am Brilliant & Beautiful!